SKOOLZ R DUMB

HOW EDUCATORS, PARENTS, AND STUDENTS CAN OUTSMART THE SYSTEM AND TAKE BACK THEIR POWER

ALIDA DAVIS ABDULLAH

BOOKLOGIX®
Alpharetta, Georgia

Although the author has made every reasonable effort to ensure that the information in this book is correct, the author does not assume and hereby disclaims any liability to any party for any loss, damage, or disruption caused by errors or omissions, whether such errors or omissions result from negligence, accident, or any other cause.

Copyright © 2025 by Alida Davis Abdullah

All rights reserved. No part of this book may be reproduced or transmitted in any form or by any means, electronic or mechanical, including photocopying, recording, or any information storage and retrieval system, without permission in writing from the author.

ISBN: 978-1-6653-0796-3 - Paperback
eISBN: 978-1-6653-0797-0 - eBook

These ISBNs are the property of BookLogix for the express purpose of sales and distribution of this title. The content of this book is the property of the copyright holder only. BookLogix does not hold any ownership of the content of this book and is not liable in any way for the materials contained within. The views and opinions expressed in this book are the property of the Author/Copyright holder, and do not necessarily reflect those of BookLogix.

Library of Congress Control Number: 2025912858

⊛This paper meets the requirements of ANSI/NISO Z39.48-1992 (Permanence of Paper)

Nikolai Pizarro contributed to Chapter 8, Whitney Austin contributed to pages 35-36; excerpts from Thom Hartmann, pages 55-57

072425

*For those who are embedded in my educational journey—
past, present, and future.*

CONTENTS

Preface		ix
Introduction		xv

PART I—SKOOLZ R . . .

Chapter 1	Pandemics R . . .	3
Chapter 2	Curricula R "Ridicula" . . .	15
Chapter 3	Systems R . . .	41
Chapter 4	Data R . . .	69

PART II—PEOPLE R . . .

Chapter 5	Administrators R . . .	87
Chapter 6	Teachers R . . .	111
Chapter 7	Parents R . . .	133
Chapter 8	Students R . . .	159
Chapter 9	We R . . .	177

Afterword	199
Acknowledgments	203
References	213

PREFACE

I get it. The title is more than controversial and I'm sure I'll get backlash from all sorts of educational experts and people who have been in the field for many years who've done their research and who are knee-deep—or should I say waist-deep or maybe even chin-deep—in education as we have come to know it. But before you come after me with your pitchforks and your torches, give this book a good read, and understand the place where it's coming from. I am the daughter, sister, niece, granddaughter, and great-niece of educators—people who spent the majority of their lives dedicated to the service of educating young people. Each of these individuals (my grandmother, her two sisters and brother-in-law, along with my father and his sister) spent thirty-plus years each—the majority of their adult lives—in the classroom and retired from the profession, so I was born with education in my bones. Amongst the six of them, a combined two hundred years was spent committed to teaching young people. My brother is twenty-plus years in the game as an educator, my husband spent more than twenty years in higher education, and I, too, have worked in various capacities as an educator over the past twenty years myself as a teacher, administrator, and advocate. So, I kinda have some credibility, even if just a little bit.

And, to be honest, I *loved* school. The wax that shined the linoleum floors and the smell of the paste they used to clean the tops of desks that emanated from the halls and classrooms at the start of the school year were like an incense to my olfactory senses. When stores stocked their shelves with brand new school supplies—pencils, pens, paper, notebooks, and binders—I bubbled with excitement. Beyond the start of the school year, I reveled in the opportunity to share my "expertise" during class discussions and in my assignments. My K–12 educational experience as a student was blissful, but it was shrouded in ignorance. Becoming a teacher during the "No Child Left Behind" era removed the scales from my eyes and helped serve as the very first spark that has resulted in the writing of this book.

There are many good schools out there and even in the worst of schools, there are some good qualities. They create social constructs for kids to find friend groups and to be exposed to people with different backgrounds from those in their immediate families and communities. For some children, schools provide a safe haven in which they can find a loving adult, comfort in their routines, and food to fill their bellies. In general, the foundational knowledge that children acquire from schools is valuable and establishes a baseline for an understanding of academic concepts that can be used in careers or when furthering their education beyond high school. However, too many schools are failing our children. Students' needs have become entangled in the weeds and over time, we have put more and more trust, finances, and resources into the schools and school systems and not enough into the *people* that make up these systems. Education has lost its human touch.

More accountability = More mandates

More achievement = More standardized tests

More innovation = More curriculum changes

In which of these equations are the *people* at the forefront? None. These are losing formulas in the equation for helping our students achieve their highest potential.

As our society, our technology, our business models, and our ability to operate globally have evolved, *people* have been the drivers of change with systems, structures, and technologies serving as the vehicles. But in education, it seems like there is much less power, autonomy, and freedom afforded to people and more emphasis being placed on systems that place mandates and restrictions on people's ability to drive education innovatively.

There are so many ways in which education should and could be advanced, such as incorporating advanced technologies or implementing fancy lessons, but without people at the forefront, none of it matters. I have seen some innovative alternatives to the traditional education model that have helped me to see the possibilities of education reform. However, the Covid-19 pandemic helped make it even more blatantly clear how important people are in making drastic changes in the way we are educating our children. We must move from a top-down, systems-centered model to a people-centered methodology, empowering the people within schools that matter the most. I have learned about student-centered and individualized learning models, but the approach I have posed within these pages focuses on ensuring *all* of us play a role in improving our schools and systems.

The infinite imaginations of students, the intelligence and expertise of teachers and administrators, and the infusion of love and nurture of parents are all instrumental in making our schools better. Consequently, the people within the schools and systems must understand their roles and do their part within educational infrastructures, working as a team to accomplish the common goal of student success. Unfortunately, the unnecessary pressures imposed by schools and school systems have led the people down a dark road. This pathway is filled with potholes of criticisms and finger-pointing, resulting in the wreckage that is teacher turnover, parent frustration, administrator burnout, and self-doubt in students.

One of the most disappointing parts of all this is that the systems have succeeded in convincing us that we the people (administrators, teachers, parents, and students) are all working *against* each other, when we are *not* (or at least, we shouldn't be). Many things have changed since I first started writing this book and initiating the process of bringing it to publication. The attack on schools has increased dramatically and there is an attack on teachers, administrators, and parents like never before. The criticisms that have been unleashed on parents by teachers, on administrators by parents, and on teachers and administrators by students is a distraction from the goal: student success.

DISCLAIMER: MUCH OF WHAT IS WRITTEN IN THIS BOOK IS BASED ON ***MY*** OWN PERSONAL EXPERIENCES. All of it is not formally research-based, although much of what I share came from information learned in classrooms, books, articles, podcasts, and (yes) even from social media. *This* is a practical layperson's guide to navigating K–12 educational systems, and it will be true to its form by being simple and easy to read. So, if you spent years in post-secondary classrooms reading academic journals and tedious hours formatting for your dissertation, you may loosen your ties and bra straps—this *ain't* that type of book. You're welcome. My goal is that this book will allow people to understand some of the challenges that exist in schools and encourage them to establish a blueprint for positive change. My hope is that this book inspires you to take actions that will help both young people and struggling schools/school districts to advance.

There are some schools out there that have built infrastructures that support diversity, holistic learning, and a challenging academic environment that sparks curiosity, creativity, critical thinking, and collaboration. These schools have the tools, but most importantly, they have the *people* who have both the skills and resources to cultivate enriching educational experiences that translate into success for students. They are not limited by political battles or restrictive legislation that takes the focus away from the people and puts a chokehold on progress. Schools of this caliber require strong intentional leadership that values the people who drive the system and doesn't allow the system to drive them. They also have resources that prevent them from being at the mercy of governmental systems and funders that require them to operate according to their own special interests in order for them to financially survive. Schools that have these characteristics are few and far between, and although every child deserves to have these experiences, many of them don't. It's heartbreaking that so many young people have spent the majority of their lives in miserable environments under miserable circumstances, all because the people don't matter to the system. It is time for that to change.

This is *my* manifesto for revolutionary change in education. Until that change comes, here is why *I* think (some) *Skoolz R Dumb*.

INTRODUCTION

WHY R SKOOLZ DUMB?

Maybe it's because I worked my behind off for school, but didn't feel like I had much to show for it by the time I graduated from college. I made all the *A*s I could possibly make and was involved in every club and organization and held almost every leadership position possible from seventh grade to my senior year in high school. I graduated second in my class and I was accepted to one of the top colleges in the nation. When this happened, I was told that "this is it"—*this* was the promised land I had worked my whole life for. I was convinced that if I graduated from there, I could do and be anything I wanted to. I believed that my degree would get me a job at a top firm and I would make plenty of money. All I had to do was walk across the stage and get that ultra-coveted piece of paper: a college degree from a prestigious institution with a great reputation. Although I received the degree, the manifestation of my dreams coming true as a result did not happen.

Perhaps this is indeed birthed out of a much deeper and more personal pain that, while others may be able to relate to, is my very own cross to bear; rooted in all the years I thought of myself as inadequate or not as smart as others because I didn't cross the threshold of a standardized test score that would have labeled me as what my state classified as "gifted." Every day in school I worked to prove that I was just as smart as the kids who got to leave their regular school environment to go to the "special" school building across town to participate in "gifted learning" once a week. Perhaps it is the deep incision that was made deeper and deeper every time I was left to wonder, "What do they do while they were there?" "Why can't I go too?" "What did the lady mean when she told my mother that I was 'too aggressive' to be a part of the gifted program?"

It could be that I didn't know or understand that the forces of racism and discrimination could have been working against me, even as a young child. I wasn't aware that when they designed the gifted eligibility tests, my ability to communicate and relate to others had not yet been considered a gift all its own and that there was no way to really test for it. I spent years struggling with my own intelligence or perceived lack of it, wondering why I was told time after time after time that I was so smart but, in my heart and mind, never feeling "good enough" because I didn't have a test score that would label me as "gifted."

The elders said, "Get your lesson!"

My parents declared, "Get good grades!"

Society exclaimed, "Get a good education!"

All the messages surrounding me proclaimed that a "good education" (whatever that meant) was the foundation of great success and that without it, you would be a failure in life. I was sold the "Education Dream," but I have buyer's remorse because I feel like I didn't get my money's worth. It was a bitter reality that smacked me in the face like a brick wall. I don't want other young people to grow up and have this awakening when they could learn the truth early in life and operate accordingly. I also don't want parents to feel like schools and the districts and systems that run them are more intelligent than they are or that they don't have the adequate knowledge and understanding for them to successfully help their children navigate. In some instances, and more recently because of laws being passed to sugarcoat the truth, many schools have a way of teaching half-truths like they are the gospel. These half-truths are barriers and they discourage people from exploring real-world knowledge with an enlightened mind once their formal education has ended. Some schools hold students hostage to the curricula and lessons that they have adopted and injuriously characterize those students based on what they know of this information. Schools and school systems have become like feeding tubes, pumping watered-down information through the valves of curricula, equipping students with just enough digestive strength to take in baby food once the tubes are disconnected. Nobody seems to be able to think for themselves anymore, everybody wants to be spoon-fed, and academic rigor comes in the form of cramming down advanced concepts only to be regurgitated on standardized tests. As long as students are insulated within the walls of an educational system, they are fine, but when it comes time to translate that into practical knowledge . . . it becomes more complicated.

I was "school smart," meaning I made good grades, was favorable in the eyes of my teachers, and had above-average test scores (yet not high enough to be considered "gifted"). Throughout my entire childhood, I was under the impression that "school smart" was going to get me where I wanted and needed to be in life, but when I reached adulthood, I learned that, sadly, it was not enough. I know now that grades and test scores are not true indicators of intelligence, but schools and school systems work to convince people that they are, and I thought that way for years before I learned differently. I have often asked myself, "How is it that deep into my adulthood, I am just now getting to the place where I am reaching my perceived potential based on how 'school smart' I was as a child?" and "How did I miss the mark of lifelong excellence and success that was 'supposed' to serve as my reward for hard work, good grades, and being involved at school?"

It could be that I just came along at the wrong time in history. We live in a world now in which you can truly be anything you want and a thirty-second video could catapult you into fame and fortune.

Perhaps if I had been able to post those old home videos on platforms that would have afforded me the opportunity to go viral, I might have already become a multimillionaire. My parents made sure that we understood we were *required* to graduate from high school and we were *required* to graduate from college and whatever we did after that was up to us. Unfortunately, learning about the arts, culture, history, and entrepreneurship wasn't encouraged in my household and as long as I got a good job with good benefits, I was doing great—but I always wanted to do *more*. For a long time, I couldn't figure out what that "more" was and even now, I'm still working to figure out how to package all my talents, interests, and experiences into a "niche" that will allow me to utilize all my gifts in a way that will also help me expand my resources in a way that blesses my family and others.

Although I didn't put in the same amount of effort in college that I had in high school, by no means was it a walk in the park to graduate—it was very difficult. But all the schoolwork I did and all the achievements I strived for in school didn't relate to a tangible career, profession, business, or money-making idea outside of school. Is making money the goal? What about making a difference? Or better yet, what about something money can't buy—peace of mind? Peace of mind about doing something I was good at and felt good about eluded me. I left high school thinking I would conquer the world and I was a good student—but what does that mean? How does that translate? My experience showed me that it doesn't automatically translate to success. Just because you're good at biology doesn't mean you will become a doctor. Doing well in your American government class doesn't automatically write you on the ballot to become a US senator. Understanding the Pythagorean theorem in your geometry class isn't necessarily going to calculate your way to a position on a NASA mission. Yet many people are under the false pretense that making good grades and doing well in class alone will convert to a high-powered job and lots of money and success. By the time I graduated from college, none of my dreams had materialized into my reality. I had gone on several job interviews for consulting and management positions to put my degree to work, but nothing came through. School, and the job search, had left me frustrated, disappointed, and (once again) feeling inadequate.

School turned me into an imposter—I was "fake smart." I knew just enough to get good grades and charm my way onto the Principal's List, but I really didn't know very much. I was underexposed and possessed an overinflated sense of my own intelligence. It was this pseudo-intellect that got me into places I didn't belong and helped "qualify" my so-called smarts through awards, achievements, and degrees. In so many instances, grades are a result of effort and *not* necessarily a measure of proficiency. So, when I found myself in the midst of true intellectuals, I felt incompetent and stupid. It has taken me many years after being out of school to learn this about myself and my experience, which is a painful and disappointing realization.

I learned the hard way that schools don't make and define people, but instead the very opposite is true. Teachers set the atmosphere in class. Parents establish the expectations they have for their children. Students apply what they are learning to achieve their own dreams and aspirations. Schools are a construct, *not* a determining measure of who we are and who we are meant to be.

People make the school. People set the tone. People are smart. Skoolz R Dumb.*

---

*For the remainder of the book, the word schools will be spelled as "skoolz" when I am referencing schools that (in my opinion) are being dumb in their approaches and decisions.

PART I
SKOOLZ R . . .

CHAPTER 1
PANDEMICS R . . .

Unprecedented. There is no better word to describe the Covid years of our lives than that one. The word unprecedented means not having done or experienced before; novel, hence the term "Novel Coronavirus" that was circulating around the start of that dreadful pandemic. It was a new thing. We have all certainly experienced the common cold, which originates from the same family of viruses as Covid-19. However, what made the disease so "new" is that unlike the common cold, Covid-19 was strange and mysterious, affecting different people in different ways and even causing the demise of some. For the common cold, runny noses, coughing, sneezing, headaches, and fever are symptoms experienced by most. But for those with Covid-19, it was unknown whether you would lose your sense of taste and smell, end up on a ventilator, pass away from it, or have no symptoms at all. It was difficult for medical experts to determine who gets what symptoms and why some people don't get any at all, despite their exposure levels. Covid-19 created a pandemic that was truly unprecedented.

Unforeseen. Prior to its start, we certainly would not have guessed at the start of 2020 a global pandemic was on the horizon. It was a milestone year in our eyes, with the promise of great things that were to happen. So many people had great hopes for the year 2020. It was an election year and the opportunity for a fresh new start in government.

It was an Olympic year, with Tokyo bringing the best and brightest in Olympic sports to the international stage. It was just a cool year in general, with digits that symbolically mean "perfect vision" *and* that are strategically lined up to make the perfect sunglasses, so people just *knew* it was going to be bright. There was no way we could have known the death, doom, and destruction that 2020 would bring. No one was prepared for the pandemic or all the issues that would take place as a result. The pandemic blindsided us all.

Unbeatable. Even years after the start of the pandemic, and with all the "progress" that has been made, it still seems as though this monster we know as Covid-19 is constantly and consistently finding ways to impact us. Unfortunately (which is another adverb that could be applied to the pandemic), Covid-19 has crept its way into every corner of our lives. It was not just a pandemic with physical and mental health impacts, this dreadful disease reverberated into our political, economic, and social lives, and continues to morph into many different strains, strands, and forms. Although many of the restrictions have been lifted, so much of what we were doing for a long time was done with a Covid-19 lens. Going to the store? Make sure you have your mask and hand sanitizer with you. Want to travel? Check to find out if your destination requires a vaccination card or negative test. Sending your kids to school? Put them in a hazmat suit and hope for the best!

Uncommon. In most of our lifetimes (with the exception of the few centenarians who were around during the Spanish flu), this is unlike anything we have ever experienced or witnessed. This required some very thorough, thoughtful, and strategic thinking on behalf of organizational leaders worldwide. Many businesses big and small had to shut down their physical operations and move to the online environment in order to sustain. They had to figure out how to maintain their supply chains, marketing efforts, and financial structures all while ensuring they kept their employees and their clientele safe from this mysterious and disruptive beast of a disease.

Healthcare systems were charged with the behemoth task of managing hospitals and emergency rooms that were starting to fill up with people severely affected by Covid, while still working to help their other patients get through illnesses that were not related to the pandemic (but could have severely impacted them had they been exposed).

Some people were dying and many people were scared. This was not a "business as usual" situation and *everybody* had to make changes—quickly *and* intelligently. With that in mind, can someone please help me understand how and why so many skoolz worked so hard to try to treat the Covid-19 pandemic in a "business as usual" manner? Of all the things the pandemic has shown us, one of them is that we can no longer approach education the way we always have. Let's be honest with ourselves and each other—many education systems have been lacking the substance necessary to truly help children grow and thrive academically for a very long time. The Covid-19 pandemic just gave us more clarity to see the *urgency* of school reform. Prior to the pandemic, many of our children were already lacking what was necessary for them to succeed educationally. However, Covid-19 exposed how skoolz have failed to provide the social, emotional, and mental support and structure necessary for children to be successful.

The Covid-19 pandemic exposed the lack of holistic support in many skoolz and the astronomical damage this has caused, not just for the individual children who have suffered through the pandemic, but for our nation and world as a whole for generations to come. That is a loaded statement and requires the dissection of layers. It also may spark controversy or, at the very least, heated arguments over what the school's role is and should be in the lives of our children. Many believe that the primary role of schools is to ensure that children are able to learn the necessary academic skills to help them become successful in college and/or their chosen career pathways. Although this may be true on the surface, we cannot ignore the fact that children are not just academic beings, but whole human beings and should be treated holistically and not just one-dimensionally. Schools are structured in ways to meet children's developmental needs from an academic perspective, which is why you see bright colors, group tables, and carpeted areas in many kindergarten classes, but a high school chemistry class will have individualized seating with a large poster of the periodic table on the wall. Unfortunately, many skoolz have missed the mark in helping students in the other aspects of their existence.

The pandemic certainly showed us that some skoolz do more to serve working parents than they do to serve children. They have become free child care, free meal service, and free transportation for people who work Monday–Friday in eight to five jobs. The parents benefit greatly, but too many children go through those skoolz for thirteen years and come out barely prepared for life beyond high school. The pandemic proved this to be true, as many parents were forced to homeschool their children while they worked their jobs from home and became quite disgruntled with the task. For those parents who were able to work remotely during this time, it became quite the balancing act to find ways to manage their work schedules and the school schedules of their children. Many became frustrated with the process of relearning old skills to help with the rigor of the academic work assigned to their children by their respective schools, while having to juggle the demands of their jobs. Some parents were able to take advantage of this time to get to know their children better and even showed their children different learning methods that were better than those they were being taught in school. During this time, some parents created their own "Homeschool Universities" and found fun ways to help their children cope with the challenging circumstances surrounding the pandemic.

When I began writing this book (it had been living rent-free in my headspace conceptually long before then), it was the middle of the summer after the sheltering in place of over 130,000 schools nationwide due to Covid-19. At that time, I was working as a public charter school teacher, with four children of my own, and the school district in which we lived had just announced their "options" for the reopening of our schools. Their so-called "options" were actually requirements that made me frustrated, hurt, angry, and disappointed for many reasons. First of all, from my vantage point, I felt like the children were being used as the pawns and guinea pigs in the economic game that our state was playing. In my opinion, the rationale for their decision to let kids go back to school was this: "If the kids go back to school, parents go back to work, and the economy can go back to normal—yay! We don't have to use taxpayer dollars to fund unemployment, and our businesses can stop bleeding out profits. Woohoo!" However, I found it interesting that a governor who wouldn't open his mansion to the public wanted to open schools so that everyone else could share their germs with each other. This was (and still is) a political game and the children are the biggest losers.

At the start of the school year, after the initial sheltering-in-place phase of the pandemic, there was a lot of talk about what is commonly referred to as Summer Slide (where students lose or forget what they've learned throughout the school year during the two and a half months of summer vacation) becoming the Covid Slide—in which they would not only have to make up for the summer months of lost learning, but also have to account for the two or three months that they missed due to sheltering in place. Sadly, all those fears and concerns about the loss of learning during this time frame are starting to present themselves in children all over the nation and quite possibly the world. However, this was a preventable phenomenon. Although we couldn't predict the pandemic, we were able to predict one of its side effects but did nothing to keep it from happening. Unfortunately, schools and school systems didn't think quickly, cohesively, or positively enough to help prevent this from becoming an all-out educational disaster.

The sheltering-in-place time-period could have served as an opportunity to shift to a more proactive approach to educating children and get ahead of the Covid Slide. However, schools are so focused on "instructional time," achieving high test scores, and ensuring that their accountability measures have been met that they couldn't think innovatively enough to help their students overcome whatever losses they were likely to experience. As a parent of four children, I knew how difficult it was to try to do my job and have them do their schoolwork too. The school where I was working had done a pretty good job of already implementing software platforms to help students improve certain skills, so getting work for my oldest son to do was easy because he attended the same school. But my daughters and youngest son were in a school that didn't know how they wanted to approach the learning process and they were all over the place. Sadly, I didn't have much time to work with any of them because of the obligations of my own job. But I wasn't discouraged because I knew that learning didn't just come from a book or computer—they learned other things and we worked through the pandemic holistically as a family.

The focus for schools should have been and should still be on how much wiser, resilient, and more intelligent our children are as a result of the pandemic, not how much learning they have lost. Part of the problem with thinking negatively about the losses and deficiencies, is that it served as a breeding ground for finger-pointing and blame-shifting. Instead, these circumstances should have allowed for schools to capitalize on those unusual circumstances to elevate children to higher levels of learning and understanding. Research from governmental agencies, nonprofits, and even Harvard have shown that children learn from playing, observing, and doing. *This* is the basic truth that should have served as guidance for ensuring that learning continued throughout the sheltering-in-place period and beyond. Regardless of people's economic circumstances, the world we live in now is centered around and is driven by access to information. Very few people in this day and age exist without a cell phone, laptop, tablet, or some other way to access digital platforms such as Google, YouTube, and the internet in general. This was a key to kids' success during the sheltering-in-place that was missed. School districts nationwide were providing laptops, tablets, and even hotspots to ensure that children had a way to access the learning that was taking place, but there were missed opportunities within this approach.

Although some students are able to afford different types of software or have more advanced access in specialized areas than others, access to information (in general) is the one "great equalizer" in our nation and world today. I often joke with people that if Google had been around when I was a kid, I would have either become a rocket scientist or found the cure to cancer by now. Today, when I need to find out something, I scour my digital devices for the answer or at least clues to the information I am seeking. Google is free. YouTube is free. Social media platforms such as Facebook, Instagram, and Twitter, are free. They are some of the greatest sources of information accessible to everyone, yet children of this generation don't even know how to properly use these resources and many skoolz are too dumb to teach it. As a matter of fact, if schools focused more on teaching kids how to *find* the information they need or want, instead of the minutiae of learning trivial facts, children would be better educated for this millennium than they currently are.

The idea of trying to conduct "Schools as Usual" during this pandemic might have been the stupidest and least productive way to attempt to educate children that we have ever seen. I mean, seriously, who *really* thought children would be focused on things that they need to learn in school without Coronavirus or Covid-19 being at the forefront of their minds? Oh, I know whose bright idea it was—the skool systems with a non-humanistic approach to educating children. They attempted to bring a traditional academic model to life in a virtual/online/distance learning environment without considering all of the social and emotional ramifications that are intertwined with this feat.

I'm no genius (at least according to the gifted standards in the state of Georgia), but if I was in charge, once schools shut down, I would have addressed remote learning as follows:

Now that we have to take our learning online, let's take this time to help guide our students like the twenty-first-century learners and leaders they already are. Many of our students are facing all kinds of challenges—economic, with some parents losing jobs and/or wages as a result of the pandemic; health, with some whose family members are becoming ill or perishing as a result of Covid-19; emotional, dealing with the fears and uncertainties of a global pandemic; physical, having to physically distance from others, wear masks, hose themselves down with Lysol, hand sanitizer, and other such disinfectants, etc. These are just a few of the ways that the Covid-19 pandemic has impacted our young people, yet we are attempting to educate them on an "as usual" basis . . . are you kidding me? The entire pandemic and consequent shutdown are a collective teachable moment that should become our impromptu/emergency curriculum to close out the school year. Yes, even for younger children, we can find ways to use this historical moment to help kids learn basic and/or complex academic topics. Statistics and probability are at the forefront and can be used to show forecasting or build models to help predict patterns of infection. Learning more about how bacteria and viruses behave serves as the perfect biology lesson. The power given to state and local governments regarding social distancing, curfews, and school closings, along with the economic impact serve as great social studies lessons. Writing an opinion essay about whether or not distance learning is working for students and families would be great for English/language arts. The impacts of the reduction of travel on the environment would make for excellent Earth science lessons. The Covid-19 pandemic could be used to teach any academic subject that exists, and who knows what level of critical thinking skills (and possible solutions for these issues) could emerge from students? Let's give this approach a try.

Sadly, we never even considered any of the aforementioned ideas as a potential overarching curriculum for all students nationwide, missing out on the possibilities of the genius solutions that our children could have provided. What if our educational leaders, with all of their glorious degrees and fabulous titles, had gotten off their high horses this one time and given the power to the kids to expose their brilliance to the world? This could have been their moment! Certainly, some kids would have completely ignored these assignments, brushed them aside, and done nothing. Some kids did that anyway, so focusing on the negative would not have made a difference. If we had actually given students the chance to save the world, they might have been able to do it. What if we had told them that their job was to connect with other children in other places and collaborate for a solution to this crazy mess? What if we said that we would take the money that was being saved from the gas we put into buses and the cost of electricity and water inside school buildings to reward them with something special if they could come up with something special? USPS, UPS, FedEx, and Amazon *never* stopped operating during that time, and schools and school districts could have partnered with these companies and/or others to come up with rewards that could have been shipped to houses or delivered digitally. To be honest, we really didn't have to have an elaborate or expensive reward—kids will do almost anything just for a piece of candy, so any small token would have sufficed. We could have come together to give the kids an assignment of a lifetime! Who knows? Within six months, perhaps this whole thing could have been over because they came up with something to get us back to normal or even better than normal. But schools and school systems spent more time debating about what distance learning should look like, how to distribute devices, and holding teachers accountable to justify their paychecks. We didn't even give our children a chance to show us what amazing concepts and new ideas could have emerged from their works—a tragedy within itself that occurs far too frequently in schools.

Schools could have united with one another to lead students to develop solutions to change our trajectory—lives could have been saved, the quality of our lives could have improved, and a whole new way of teaching and learning could have emerged as a result. You mean to tell me that even with all of the education and schooling teachers and administrators possess (master's/specialist/doctorate degrees) *nobody* could come up with a curriculum innovative enough to keep kids engaged in their academic learning *and* make an impact on our world? With all the time and energy that people in education spend in a classroom themselves to earn their degrees, you would think *somebody* would think innovatively enough to shift the focus from the "same old, same old" to allow kids to express their true genius by giving them assignments that are relevant, meaningful, and potentially life-changing. This baffles me.

During the shutdown, some people would say stuff like, "Many kids don't have access to computers or the internet." This was a fact, but it's a terrible copout because the last time I checked, Ticonderoga, Bic, and Mead were all still manufacturing pencils, pens, and paper. And if you think that writing on paper is obsolete, feel free to research the countless numbers of companies that are *selling out* of journals, calendars, and notepads. On top of that, our learning experiences should not be limited to classroom settings. No longer do we live in a day and age where we have to go to the library, summon the media specialist, and access knowledge via microfiche or the Dewey decimal system. If you want to learn about something, there is knowledge *everywhere*, literally right in the palms of our hands. Very few people are without cell phones or access to them and if you want to know something, all you have to do is type it in your browser to find out more.

For children who were without a smartphone, tablet, or computer, it didn't mean that they couldn't have taken advantage of the learning right within their own environments. The sheltering-in-place period occurred in the spring of the year, and although the snow may have barely been melting in some places, many places had weather decent enough to go outside, even if just for a little while. All people (young and old) can become observers of the world around them to gain knowledge and sometimes just a simple conversation can turn into a teachable moment and learning opportunity. The pandemic and everything that came along with it could have been easily transformed to help kids learn as much as they could during this very difficult time. And if the pandemic wasn't enough, the unrest that occurred in the aftermath of the murders of Ahmaud Arbery, George Floyd, and Breonna Taylor were curricula all their own to explore. On the surface alone, these events are what social studies lessons are made of, but when we look more deeply, they are also interdisciplinary as their impact reaches far beyond civics and government classes.

As fast as other industries moved during the pandemic's sheltering-in-place period in order to meet the needs and demands of their constituents, education moved way too slowly and not collaboratively or creatively enough to produce favorable outcomes for students. Schools allowed for the Covid-19 pandemic shutdown to become the greatest *missed* teachable moment in modern history! The incompetent nature of some skoolz and skool systems was not only demonstrated through their inability to find a way to make academic subjects salient in a distance learning environment, but also through their failure to reopen schools in a way that would keep students and teachers safe. Everything became politicized and nobody could seem to make concrete, research-based decisions about mask mandates, physical distancing, and vaccination requirements. It was a hot mess and exposed just how dumb some skoolz really are!

CHAPTER 2
CURRICULA R "RIDICULA" . . .

A nd traditional methods of instruction are often ineffective. When did learning become so difficult? Why don't we trust children's ability to learn organically, just as they did in their early years? Is learning really hard or has boring, mundane irrelevant curricula and ineffective methodologies of teaching made it a challenge that doesn't have to exist? When babies are born, they are helpless. They can hear, but can barely see, they can't walk, and they communicate through crying. They are primitive, sensory beings able only to learn through their basic human/physical senses (taste, touch, smell, hearing, and sight). As they develop and are able to do more, they somehow miraculously learn without someone "teaching" them how to do so. Nobody ever says, "Your grandmamma taught you how to walk," or "Your brother taught you how to talk," because these are "learned" not "taught" skills. Once these skills were learned, they were perfected because we exercise them every single day in almost every waking moment of our lives.

A curriculum is defined as "the regular or a particular course of study in a school, college, etc.," according to dictionary.com. There are so many aspects and types of curricula that could be examined, but in this chapter, they have been narrowed down to the following: the role of nurture in the advancement of learning, speed/pacing of instruction, mastery of content, and relevance to real-world experiences. It is my hope that by looking specifically at these aspects of curricula, we will change the way kids learn for the better.

THE ROLE OF NURTURE IN THE ADVANCEMENT OF LEARNING

We don't take our babies to a cold building with other babies and say to them, "Today, we are going to learn how to walk, talk, etc." Their entire process of learning comes by way of two primary means: nurturing/love and observation/modeling. Although the gateway to acquiring these skills is through babies' physical senses, the vehicles are admiration for the child and a genuine desire for them to grow. A by-product of our admiration for children is touch. Have you ever seen a cute baby and just want to squeeze their cheeks or give them a big hug? Or noticed that in many hospitals and birthing centers, the "Golden Hour" has been established in which newborn babies are placed on their parents' bare chests for their very first skin-to-skin experiences?

Touch is incredibly powerful and can have long-lasting impacts, depending upon a person's experience with touch or lack thereof. In particular, touch (or lack of touch) can significantly affect an infant's development and cognitive abilities as they grow older. When I worked at a tutoring center, I remember a family of children who had been refugees and were adopted from a country in Europe, which alone is a terrible childhood trauma that they had to overcome. One of the children in particular had severe developmental delays and was not learning at a rate comparable to his peers. I found out that he was abandoned as a baby, and missed out on critical moments in which he should have been held, cuddled, and cradled by loving adults. Consequently, this lack of nurture prevented his brain from developing properly, and I was shocked when I learned this!

An article written by Harriet Dempsey-Jones, a postdoctoral researcher in clinical sciences at the University of Oxford, on a website called The Conversation shares the value and impact of human touch during babies' formative years. She writes about a study done by a team of researchers led by Nathalie Maitre, conducted at the Nationwide Children's Hospital in Columbus, Ohio. Approximately 125 babies were outfitted with electrodes to measure brain activity when touched. They noted significant differences between full-term and premature babies (those born prior to thirty-seven weeks of gestation). They found that premature babies had markedly reduced brain activity when touched compared to full-term babies. However, it was their findings with positive versus negative touch that stood out most to me:

> The researchers also showed, for the first time, that for premature babies, the quality of touch while in hospital after birth (typically around one month) affected the functioning of the babies' brains. When they tested the premature babies, just before they were discharged from the hospital, they found that the more they experienced pleasant, nurturing touch (such as breastfeeding or skin contact) the greater the brain response to touch. Conversely, unpleasant touch, such as skin punctures and tube insertions, were associated with reduced brain activity.

This demonstrates that our sensory experiences in early life have important effects on brain function. Maitre's findings add to the growing understanding that the functioning of the brain cannot be considered separately to that of the body.

Besides human touch, negative experiences in general can not only affect cognitive ability, but also create health problems in people. ACEs (Adverse Childhood Experiences) is an indicator of the health problems that can occur in adulthood based on the adverse childhood experiences that someone has had, including, according to the Centers for Disease Control (CDC), Adverse Childhood experiences are defined as: "Potentially traumatic events that occur in childhood (ages zero–seventeen) such as experiencing violence, abuse, or neglect; witnessing violence in the home or community; having a family member attempt or die by suicide . . . [are] linked to health problems, mental illness, and substance use problems in adulthood.

I have been fortunate enough to learn firsthand how positive and enjoyable learning experiences can have a huge influence on how much information is retained during that time. Some of my best and most favorite learning experiences occurred during my two years of junior high school. I was in an academically rigorous environment that also built in wholistic social and emotional experiences that provided me with a strong educational foundation that carried me through high school and beyond. Likewise, one of my former students, who is like a son to me, shares on many occasions almost verbatim the lessons I was teaching while he was in my seventh-grade language arts class. He has told me on numerous occasions how that time period in his life represented some of his happiest moments. The life lessons as well as the language arts lessons were etched in his mind and were able to make an impact on his life, which should be the goal of education anyway. Unfortunately, some kids can't get to the lessons being taught *in* the classroom because they are struggling to get through the pain they are suffering in their lives *beyond* the classroom.

With infants, we mostly let them *be* and somehow within a matter of a year and a half to two years, they learn to walk, communicate both nonverbally and verbally, and how to interact with others. And they *master* these tasks through continued *practice*, time after time. They continue learning in this way, even if they don't go to a school, daycare, or a learning center. But when they get to kindergarten they are trained and conditioned to remain in a box, sit still, be quiet, get in a line, and "learn" what is taught based on a prescribed set of rules and guidelines. While these rituals may be limiting, kindergartners are loved and nurtured by a teacher and sometimes a teacher's assistant, and a form of this nurturing continues until kids reach about third or fourth grade. Interestingly enough, this is around the same time kids, especially boys (and in particular Black and Brown boys), begin to lose interest in school. Could it be that over time, as there is gradually less nurturing in a classroom, kids are less "attracted" to learning?

The Covid-19 pandemic taught us that children need the nurturing and love of their teachers as much as, if not more than, the academic content that is offered. Certainly, quality instruction of subjects is important and can even be taught online, as evidenced by the many distance-learning opportunities that exist in both academia and the general marketplace. However, this approach does not generally translate into a quality holistic learning experience for *children*. It is clear that the expressions of body language and visual cues that exist in an in-person environment are what help kids develop healthily. Direct eye contact, tone of voice, and presence of being were the greatest losses in the distance learning paradigm. During the virtual learning sessions of my then-kindergarten-aged son, I recall him wanting to do the assignments and complete the work, but seemed to feel "violated" by being "watched" through the screen and refused to do the work during the live sessions. It was an unnatural interaction and his apprehension led to a lack of performance on his behalf.

In my personal observations, I have noticed how some homeschooled children perform much better than their peers who go to school every day. When I have taught students who came from homeschool environments, they were so much more focused and they demonstrated behaviors that indicated they were truly interested in what was being taught. Many homeschooled children place at the top levels in geography and spelling bees and when tested for proficiency, some outscore many others who have been taught in traditional learning environments. Some of their parents are not certified teachers and have not obtained the higher levels of formal training many school teachers may have. However, their homes and academic instruction are filled with nurture and love, which *could* be responsible for higher academic achievement and performance in their children. Whenever students are in classrooms in which they don't receive adequate emotional nurturing and are deprived of this important element in their learning experience, it leads to academic inadequacies.

From kindergarten until about second or third grade, kids are nurtured and loved on—they're cute, they're sweet, and they're adorable—so teachers and schools treat them as such. In kindergarten, much of the instruction is presented with fun games, bright photos, and whimsical songs. By the time they get to the third grade, however, schools and teachers shift gears and students have to "tighten up" and learn how to "handle their business." One of the warnings and disclaimers kids get at the beginning of their fourth-grade school year is, "We are not going to 'baby' you anymore." It's no wonder that fourth and fifth grades are the years students begin to lose interest in school. Furthermore, many kids enter the fourth grade without being taught the executive functioning skills necessary to help them be successful with their newfound expectations of independence. This certainly places kids at a disadvantage, and we don't give kids the fair chance they need to provide a strong framework for their educational well-being.

PACING OF INSTRUCTION VS. MASTERY

Is it nurture alone that causes homeschooled students to excel academically, or is it the pace at which they learn? In many homeschool environments, students are allowed to pace themselves in order to gain true mastery of fundamental skills and concepts. Parents are working directly with their children in an individualized setting, so they can recognize when their children are stuck or struggling with a concept. Because they are not bound by time constraints and the pressure to just keep moving forward regardless of where students are, homeschooling parents and facilitators are able to slow down and provide students with the support necessary to overcome academic challenges. It is not until they have fully gained an understanding of these areas, that they move on to the next, which makes advanced concepts much easier for them to comprehend.

When my daughter was in the fourth grade, she complained to me that just as she was learning one mathematical concept, the teacher and class moved on to something else. In math, they were zooming through the curriculum without ensuring that students had a full understanding of what they were supposed to be learning before moving on to the next lesson or unit. As a result, my daughter began to feel inferior and unintelligent because, by the time she was starting to get the hang of one concept, it was time to move on to something else. What are schools in such a rush for?

Can somebody please help me understand why schools are pressuring teachers to blitz through curricula like a linebacker trying to get to the quarterback on a third-down play in a football game? Is this the reason why students are not mastering concepts as they should? There are foundational concepts in reading, writing, and math that all of the other, more complex subjects are built upon and should be mastered. Why are we not demanding and ensuring that the mastery of these concepts takes place? What good is it to glaze over basic foundational concepts that should be mastered just for the sake of saying that our kids are learning more advanced concepts? Why are there high school students taking Algebra, Geometry, and Calculus, who barely know their times tables or how to calculate fractions?

Why do we put so much emphasis on advancing kids to the next level without ensuring they have mastered the level they are on? When teaching someone how to ride a bicycle, we don't get them just to the place where the training wheels come off and then expect them to ride the bike lane on busy streets. It takes a level of maturity, understanding, and the ability to connect the dots to advance when learning a new skill. So why do the "timelines" of curricula prevent kids from properly processing basic concepts before advancing them to higher levels? There is no way we can expect that they will fully learn, remember, and understand what they have been taught with this kind of "speed teaching" going on.

It is more important for a child to *master* fundamental concepts, even if it compromises their opportunity to learn more advanced concepts during that particular time period or school year. This will help to ensure that when students are finally introduced to advanced levels of the subject material, they will be prepared and (in many cases) have a knowledge base solid enough to accelerate through it. In my opinion, this is much more effective than exposing students to higher-level concepts without them having a full understanding of their corresponding core components. If children can read *well* (and comprehend what they're reading), and have a *strong* foundational understanding of basic computation (adding, subtracting, multiplying, and dividing), there's nothing they can't learn. Isn't that what *scaffolding* is all about—taking what you know (and have *mastered*) and building upon it to learn a more advanced concept? Adding is a simplified version of multiplication, subtraction is a simplified version of division, fractions are division problems, and math skills build from there. But when you don't have a good grasp of the basics, no matter how many advanced concepts you introduce, they won't stick. I've seen it far too often that kids who are struggling in math by the time they reach middle school and/or high school didn't learn their multiplication tables.

Just as it is important for kids to master fundamental concepts to have a frame of reference for what they will learn in the future, it is also vital to know they don't have to master *everything*. All things are not meant to be mastered, and to do so would be a waste of time. It requires discernment and intelligence to know what we should spend time getting students to master versus what they should merely be exposed to. Certainly, some kids will be more interested and passionate about some materials over others, and for those children who want to master a certain topic or concept, their thirst should not be quenched. However, to have droves of kids mass-memorizing stuff that can be easily referenced is a poor use of the instructional time that schools seem to value so greatly.

Back in the day (prior to the internet and social media), we didn't have constant access to information and data the way we do now, so we *had* to memorize facts and become masters of information in order to be proficient at the next level. However, data is so much more easily accessible than it was back then. For example, all the United States presidents from George Washington up to the present are something we can find out within a matter of seconds just by entering the right information in an internet search engine. It's great for quiz shows such as *Jeopardy!* or for trivia games, but it is nonessential to our everyday lives. This is not something we should require kids to master or memorize. However, if a student really enjoys learning about them, then fine—they should be encouraged to do so, but the curriculum shouldn't prioritize it. That is just one example, but there are so many areas within curricula in which the focus is on mastering content that should be referenced on an as-needed basis.

Much of what is being learned in school can be discovered easily through the many media sources readily available to each of us in the palm of our hands, but students barely know how to access it. This is one of the ways in which many schools have remained antiquated and have not advanced with technology. They continue to enforce the mastery of subject matter that should instead be referenced. Showing kids *how* and *where* to find the information they need as well as how to discern fact from fiction is just as, if not more, important than teaching them *what* to learn. Additionally, teaching kids how to process what they've learned will help them to successfully complete their classroom assignments in the present *and* facilitate their ability to implement knowledge they obtain in the future. Even doctors and lawyers who go to school for years often refer back to manuals and journals when they need to—nobody remembers *everything* they learned in school! Why don't we teach and train kids how to effectively acquire data for themselves instead of just shoving what we think they should know down their throats?

REAL-WORLD APPLICATION OF CURRICULA

When it comes to school knowledge, how much of it do we really need to use after we have left the confines of classrooms to navigate our lives as adults? I would argue not much.

I attended a conference in which Nathan Rossi, motivational speaker and founder of Recalibrate 360, asked the crowd three questions:

1) "In school, how many of you took a class called 'How to make lots of money'?" (Almost no one raised their hand.)

2) "How many learned to dissect a frog?" (The room was filled with people who had their hands raised.)

3) "How's that working out for you?" (Whispers and murmurs reverberated through the room.)

In the twenty-first century, you can make millions of dollars just by creating a silly thirty-second video. Thanks to major advancements in digital media, you can truly *do* and *be* anything you want, without having to go to school for years just to accomplish it. For example, a person interested in finances (the stock market, cryptocurrencies, and the like) no longer has to obtain an MBA from a prestigious business school just to become an "expert." They can literally tap into the world of the internet, YouTube, and read books from other experts, interpret the information they've obtained, and apply it in a way to grow their own finances, and *voila!*—a financial expert is born. Better yet, that same person doesn't even have to interpret or apply the knowledge in their own life. They could literally just go get the information and start sharing it. If enough people are interested and want to keep getting more, they gain popularity and get paid just for giving away free knowledge! With all of this going on, how are schools being effective by teaching the tired, outdated information that's loaded in most curricula? They are not.

Some curricula focus too much on the what instead of the how, leaving out the relevance of the material being taught and how it relates to real life or teaching concepts for the sake of saying that your students are "advanced," but never apply what they've learned to real life. Some examples of this include forcing kids to learn technical jargon that doesn't relate to how to actually utilize the concept being taught. (How many of you can't remember what a "gerund" is but apply the words building, swimming, telling, and flying perfectly?) We spend too much time on topic knowledge that equates to very little in everyday life, but not enough time ensuring that kids know concepts they will use all the time. Can somebody please help me understand why we drill kids how to plot a graph, but the basics (multiplication facts and basic number sense) have been skimmed over? This approach to implementing curricula does two things: robs kids of knowledge that is valuable to their well-being in their adulthood and in some cases, causes a sense of boredom with what they are learning. How many times have you or your children asked the age-old question, "How is (fill in the blank with whatever concept they are learning) going to help me in real life?"

What if school curricula went through a major overhaul and was updated for twenty-first-century success? What would it look like? What would kids learn? What would be the best way to approach this content with students? Well, here are a few ideas:

READING

Reading is fundamental—and that's not just a slogan! We often use this phrase loosely or in a joking manner, but this is probably one of the truest and most serious statements ever made. Reading is fundamental for every single subject that exists and it is upon literacy that knowledge hinges. Certainly, we can listen to books or podcasts, but so much of what we hear is based upon what is written that even listening can be considered synonymous with reading. If you can read, there is nothing you can't learn. A person can be truly self-taught if they know how to read. Although digital forms of information and data exist in the form of pictures and videos, it is difficult to obtain true and in-depth knowledge without being able to read and gain understanding through written words. Math, science, social studies, and language arts can all be learned just from reading, so reading comprehension may be the single most important academic skill we can teach to children. If nothing else is done well or done right, reading is the one discipline that must be mastered by students in order for them to successfully navigate through life (at least in many Western civilizations).

I believe that even if kids only focused on reading from the time they entered kindergarten until the time they graduated high school, many of them could be better off in some cases than they are now. This may come with a lot of pushback and disagreement, but think about it. If we work diligently with young people from the very beginning to fully comprehend what they are reading and give them the tools to discover what they don't already know (i.e. new vocabulary, researching new concepts) as they matriculate, they will have the keys to the gateway of the world. They could read about history, finances, and whatever other subject they are interested in and can become experts in just about anything. Too many times, the answers that people are looking for can be found simply by reading information and being able to comprehend and apply the content that has been read.

MATH/ELA

Many may think that math and English/language arts are on two opposite sides of the academic spectrum, but they are more closely related than people may realize. One of the greatest areas of weakness when kids are learning math is word problems. The key to those word problems is not the math, but in understanding what the question is asking them to do. Most children can effectively add three plus four and come up with seven, but when you wrap those numbers in a scenario that requires them to figure out how three apples and four oranges in a basket are a total of seven pieces of fruit, then the task becomes more complex. However, this is the way math problems actually occur in real life. When cooking a recipe, there is no laid-out equation or computational problem that is given for you to start solving. Instead, you have to ask yourself questions in order to arrive at the computations to help you achieve your desired results. Is the recipe in metric form and do I have to convert it to imperial measurements? Is the recipe too big or too small for the number of people I am trying to feed? Can I effectively substitute one ingredient for another and if so, what measurements are required to do so? The same is true for working with your personal finances, planning an event or trip, and the many tasks we do in life that require math skills.

Almost every math problem encountered in the real world is a word problem, so why are more curricula not designed to help kids master this very important skill from the very beginning? We show kids letters and numbers separately, without bridging the two from the start, making kids feel as though they operate and exist without each other. This is a flawed approach because numbers in the real world make no sense without context and it robs children of the opportunity to build critical thinking skills involving mathematical concepts. When people ask what time it is, they want to have an idea of how much time has passed since a particular event or how much time they have before an event begins. When asking about how much an item costs, people are calculating whether or not they have enough to cover the price or to determine the value versus the monetary amount assigned to it. In the real world, numbers and math-related scenarios don't exist as just numbers floating around as computational sentences and equations—they have meaning! With that in mind, students should be taught number sense and how to solve math problems in conjunction with reading and sentence structure. Unfortunately, it's easier just to create simple computation problems than to take the time to craft those that require adding relevance to the numbers, so it can cause kids to struggle with word problems in school and eventually with critical thinking skills in life.

On another note, separating math and English/language arts, I really need to know the answer to this one question: What is the obsession with teaching the coordinate plane and related concepts in math? When I was growing up, I only remember this being something that was touched on briefly, but we focused on other math skills. However, in recent years, it appears that this math concept comes up more frequently than I ever recall encountering it as a student. The worst thing about this concept is the amount of time spent trying to get kids to learn and understand it versus the amount it is actually used in the real world. Certainly, if you are seeking a career in engineering or maybe even architecture, learning this could be incredibly useful. However, in all of my many jobs and endeavors throughout my life, I have never used a coordinate plane to solve problems. As a matter of fact, I have never even thought about using it as a problem-solving tool. Maybe the "National Council of Teachers of Mathematics," or whoever determines such content, can help me understand the rhyme or reason, but in my opinion, this is yet another learning concept that shouldn't be taught unless absolutely necessary. I mean, what is really the point? Help me out here!

SOCIAL STUDIES

Social studies is everywhere and all around us. All of the things that go on around us at any given time could and *should* be taught as a social studies curriculum. No textbook is needed for this subject! Newspapers, podcasts, and social media are all tools that could be used to teach social studies. The global Covid-19 pandemic; the murders of George Floyd, Breonna Taylor, and Ahmaud Arbery and their corresponding trials; supply-chain issues; climate change and global warming; and the housing and real estate markets are all topics that could be easily explored in a social studies class. This is a place for children to utilize their knowledge base and imagination to help solve the nation's and world's problems. Traditionally, history is taught chronologically in a vacuum with no context or tie-in to what's happening in modern times so, for many students, it could be perceived as boring and irrelevant. Social studies should be taught from an interdisciplinary perspective, bringing the concepts of history, government, civics, economics, and geography together in a fun and interesting way that helps kids see their place in our society and world. It has to be connected to who they are and where they are in order for it to make sense to them, so tie it all together instead of keeping it all separated. For example, it would have been great if children were taught that the reason why it was difficult to get a PS5 (or why the price went up on them) during the pandemic is because of the domino effect of the pandemic on supply chain issues in places like Japan where many of their components are manufactured. This will help them understand how and why broad global issues make an impact on their individual lives.

SCIENCE

Here is a little "food for thought": The top two leading causes of death are heart disease and cancer. In recent years, we have learned more about how these illnesses can be prevented, treated, and even reversed through proper diet, exercise, and maintaining healthy stress levels. Yet in thirteen years of school (at least in the state of Georgia and many others also), only one semester is devoted specifically to health. Even in the twelve years that medical doctors spend in prestigious and academically rigorous programs, only one semester—or at most one year—of coursework in nutrition is required. We spend a whole year of school taking biology, but a very small portion of that course is committed to the biology of humans and how we can improve our own lives for the better. We learn about protozoa, the anatomy of a plant cell, the classification system, but none of that class is truly committed to how we can improve our well-being through understanding how our bodies function and what they need to operate at optimal levels. In chemistry classes, we learn all about the periodic table, but in none of my chemistry classes did I learn how magnesium (Mg, atomic number 12) works with phosphorus (P, atomic number 15) and calcium (Ca, atomic number 20) to give bones their strength and structure. I certainly didn't learn about the proton pump in the kidneys that helps filter potassium (K, atomic number 19) and sodium (Na, atomic number 11) in and out of the nephrons in the kidney to create homeostasis. These concepts are important to help understand the importance of these nutrients when preventing or treating osteoporosis and hypertension, among other preventable health conditions, yet they are very rarely taught in a general chemistry class. (Strangely enough, however, I *was* required to learn those abbreviations and atomic numbers—which by the way I never used beyond my required freshman chemistry class in college and in the words I'm writing right now.)

In a lecture by Andrea Nakayama, founder of the Functional Nutrition Alliance in Portland, Oregon, she was breaking down the effects of refined sugar on the body and she said:

> It is good to note, in terms of chemistry and how our body processes different foods, that such a small structural difference [in this case she was referring to the similarity of glucose to galactose]—what it is here is a cis instead of a trans structure—the direction in which one of the atoms is facing. That difference can make a huge difference in terms of digestion. I always think this is interesting because I had someone ask me, "Oh that's curious that you look at nutrition in terms of chemistry." And I thought, *Hmmm, it's curious that that would be a question*, because nutrition *is* chemistry. Everything happening in your body is chemistry. There is a chemical reaction.

As a matter of fact, if the only science we ever learned was about the human body—the chemistry, the biology, the anatomy, and the physiology that all takes place in our bodily systems—and mastered them, we would have enough content to take us all the way through college and med school. With this level of knowledge about ourselves, we might be able to revolutionize the healthcare industry and have the wisdom necessary to no longer need it in the same way we do now—hmmm, imagine that!

AND THEN THERE'S SAM (SPORTS, ARTS, AND MUSIC)

Although these three cocurricular areas have become greatly minimized within many schools and school systems over time, I am keenly aware of their importance in the educational landscape. I am going to call these disciplines "Big SAM" to describe them, because schools should recognize them as incredibly valuable to students' educational experiences and they should be prioritized greatly. For many children, Big SAM provides social-emotional support and a sense of purpose that can't always be found in classes focused on academic subjects. I am going to challenge the thinking of those who feel as though traditional academic subjects reign supreme in the realm of education. If schools are to be truly innovative, it starts with rethinking what is being taught and the way that curricula are presented. I have shared how curricula for academics could be implemented for effectiveness and mastery, but in this section, I want to take it a bit further by showing how Big SAM could be leveraged and why it could be the most profound teaching approach of them all.

Let's think for a moment that Big SAM was at the forefront of teaching and learning. Students walk into a building filled with artwork on the walls (created by students, of course), hear band, orchestral, and choral music being pumped throughout the building, and have sports programs that are prioritized with state-of-the-art facilities to advance their participation. Unfortunately, some schools possess some of the aforementioned facilities and the bells and whistles that go along with them, but they miss the mark when it comes to holistically incorporating Big SAM into curricula. But what if there were school curricula built around Big SAM? How could we bring something like this to life and what would it look like?

SPORTS

One of my former students absolutely could not sit still, was disruptive, and was unengaged in my class—all he wanted to do was play basketball. I got this crazy idea that maybe if I just let him learn and improve his math skills using basketball, he might actually learn more. My class, "math support," was considered a "special" (many PE, music, arts, and foreign language classes are defined in this way), so one day I was able to coordinate with the PE teacher to have him go to the gym to reinforce his understanding of ratios. He had to shoot a certain number of baskets per round in comparison with another student or the PE teacher, then determine the ratios of shots taken versus made. He completed the work beautifully and I loved that he learned something and was truly engaged in the learning process. At the same time, I was discouraged because I knew this was not something I could let him do every day. This was not a practice that would be allowed and there was no way I could monitor him while he was in the gym and the rest of the class was with me. But what if I could? What if this was the curriculum for every child who was motivated and engaged by sports? What if we could take those kids out to the football and baseball fields or set them up in basketball and volleyball gyms and allow them to use the sports to learn everything else? I still distinctly remember "Donald in Mathmagic Land," which was a Donald Duck cartoon released in 1959—more than sixty years ago—that explained how math was incorporated in almost every popular sport that exists. I need help understanding why we haven't expanded this idea to help meet the needs of students who thrive in—or have an interest in—sports? Why not create math problems that explore the different ways two teams could end up with their final scores and have students explain how they reached their solutions? Or have students write an inspirational voiceover to coincide with a story about an athlete or sports team that they admire? What about having students explore the many ways that sports have been at the forefront of social justice issues? Why does this seem like such a difficult concept to implement?

There are so many young people who are truly motivated by sports and dance (for the record, I count dancers as athletes too), that it's pretty foolish to me that more curricula are not centered around sports. Instead of kids reading stories or doing word problems *about* sports, why not have kids *doing* the sports to help them learn about other academic subjects?

ART

Visual art is a subject that is either not taught well or not taught at all in many schools. However, visual arts could be utilized innovatively to teach other disciplines. With art, it is important to think "beyond the canvas" and not limit art education to just crayons, copy paper, and popsicle-stick crafts. All too often, art class is basically crafting without context, without proper techniques, and without connection to the real world, or it is learning *about* art and artists without actually *doing* any art. Art is so much deeper than the way it is often taught in many schools. Showing students how to implement the principles of design, elements of art, and the utilization of high-quality art tools, while learning professional art techniques that yield magnificent pieces of art helps students think more creatively and see the world more beautifully. When these opportunities are either watered down or completely removed from traditional school environments, we rob children of their ability to expand their sense of imagination to create works that could potentially change the world.

Similar to sports, visual arts are a great way to teach the other disciplines, such as math, language arts, social studies, and science. There are so many connections between the various areas of art to academic disciplines that it is an unfortunate shame art is not being utilized in this way. A friend of mine is a phenomenal artist who uses his works to serve as a teaching tool for history. He takes historical accounts and significant figures in history and weaves them together, using them as a teaching tool. Another art teacher I know uses what kids are learning in their reading classes and connects those lessons to art history as they create meaningful masterpieces using professional artist-level tools and techniques. She also helps her students see art in the world around them and teaches them the importance of design in all that they do. This is a rare occurrence in many art classes, but by implementing these types of strategies more universally, the spaces in which we live and exist could be a much more beautiful (and well-designed) place!

The saddest thing about my art experience in my K–12 years as a student is that I left the class hating it. Before I got to the seventh grade, I remember spending some of my free time drawing figures and faces thinking I would enhance my skills by actually taking an art class. Instead, the exact opposite happened. I have never considered myself someone who is into social studies or history, so to learn about Picasso, Van Gogh, and Leonardo Da Vinci without actually *doing* any art was a complete turnoff. I was a creative writer and even enjoyed design—projects were always my thing—but my art class was less than ideal. I don't recall learning to *do* any art and never considered exploring my more creative inclinations because I was so discouraged by my junior high art class. This was an entire area of learning I missed out on because it wasn't presented in an engaging way in school, which happens far too frequently in all subjects, not just in art. Learning more about art from a design perspective is not just to make things aesthetically appealing, but it also aids in helping people understand spatial concepts and even function. Art and design as a collective is the foundation of so many exploits we will undergo in our everyday lives that it's a shame we don't teach it more often and in a way that benefits people beyond the classroom.

For a long time, I would hear people discourage those who were naturally gifted artists and lead them to pursue other career pathways to more "secure" income-generating jobs, careers, and businesses. "You don't want to live on the street," and "What if there is no market for your art?" are some of the statements I would hear when kids would talk about their desire to become artists in the future. Well, thanks to

Non-Fungible Tokens (NFTs) and access to global markets through the internet and social media, "starving artists" can become a thing of the past. As a result, we should be implementing art programs in schools like never before and helping kids utilize their skills and talents to create works that will impact the world.

Around 2015 or 2016, I started following an amazing artist on Instagram by the name of Whitney Austin (@whitney_austin). I loved her artwork and not only did I think she was talented, but I was certain she had been trained and doing art her whole life, until she posted the following:

Photo Caption by Whitney Austin: I didn't go to college for art, & I have only been painting for 3 years now . . . as a child I only felt comfortable with drawing but did that stop me from learning how to paint? Naaaaahhh!

Comments: Let me tell you! I never went to college for art, and actually, the last time I took an art class was in high school . . . over 13 years ago! So of course at 27, I didn't think that I still had the skill to create . . . or even come close to making a few bucks off of it lol. I only felt comfortable with drawing, so me painting was something completely new for me! I remember shopping at Michaels to buy my first set of paintbrushes and cheap paint lol. I made soooo many mistakes and got frustrated sooooooo much omg!! It took me a while to feel comfortable enough to even share my artwork to my friends. My paintings in my eyes wasn't "good enough" to make money from. It wasn't until I finally started to practice with my brushes, mixing colors, and building layers . . . that I felt cool with claiming that art was a hobby of mine. I felt confident enough to tell people and share what I created . . . and that's how the world slowly started to see my work. Each time I created I became a little more sure that I still had talent from all these years and that there was a possibility of it becoming more lucrative. So what changed me?? MY MINDSET! I had to remind myself that it's ok if painting is new to me, it's ok if I haven't done any art in almost 10 years, it's ok if my work is only being sold for $50 . . . I saw that each painting was just another step getting closer to my dream! I built my own goals for myself, without comparing my work to others and without feeling unsure that at almost 27 I was finally figuring out what I wanted to do! CHANGE YOUR MINDSET and don't be scared to take a few steps back to learn something new, to propel your future! I still am amazed at how far God has taken me with my gift and how I continue to grow as an artist . . . but one thing is for sure . . . I didn't start to become successful until I recognized myself as an artist and not someone who just paints on the side for fun. BELIEVE IN YOURSELF, TEACH YOURSELF, and APPLY YOURSELF! I started to paint in 2015 but just opened my 2nd art gallery and touring nationally to teach art to others . . . IF I CAN DO IT WITHOUT ANY EXPERIENCE, YOU CAN!!! NOW GO BE GREAT AND CHANGE YOUR MINDSET!

What if Whitney Austin allowed the limitations of what she learned within the confines of her school to prevent her from becoming the artist she has blossomed into? What if she didn't believe enough in herself to keep going because her school experiences didn't push her to pursue her dreams? As you read, she had learned how to draw, but didn't experiment with paint and focus on becoming the artist that she is until she was twenty-seven years old! Schools should be a place to *inspire*, not a place to send dreams to *expire*. For many students, when a quality art curriculum isn't a part of their academic experience, their creative drive dies. We must work to change skoolz so that the premature deaths of creativity can stop.

MUSIC

The headline read "Want Smarter Kids? Teach Music Not Coding, according to MIT" in an article written by Geoffrey James, Contributing Editor at Inc. Magazine, and I was instantly intrigued. I had already heard that playing music to unborn babies in utero helped evolve and develop their brains, but I had not heard that music was preferential to coding for children. In a study conducted at the University of Zurich, it was discovered that, "Learning music early in life makes the brain more connected, inducing neural plasticity capable of improving neurological capabilities beyond music." This study showed that even if a child does not continue their music studies or play an instrument, the benefits remain beyond those lessons. Although I have never met any of the study's participants, I can bet that some of those who were classified as musicians are brilliant. During my early twenties, I had the good fortune of getting to know some of the most talented artists in the music industry. Some of them had been playing instruments since they were young and knew how to produce and arrange music, while others used their voices as instruments. Many of them had gone to college and majored in disciplines outside of music, but in their hearts and souls, they wanted to follow their musical calling. They left their academic pursuits to achieve their goals and dreams in music and never looked back. These musicians are now well-respected and are quite successful. Additionally, there is a population of musical talents who used their musical careers as a platform to become successful outside of their music careers, which is an indication that getting a diploma or degree doesn't determine their destiny for greatness.

In no way am I advocating for dropping out of high school or college, but what I am saying is that if skoolz established programs for students whose focus is on Big SAM, with a curricular emphasis on practicalities instead of technicalities, then perhaps dropping out would be unnecessary. Why couldn't we extend course credit to young prodigies using studio time, getting songwriting credits, and working with industry giants (similar to an internship)? Unfortunately, in some cases, the difference between those who drop out of high school or college is a credit or two in some mandated class that has very little (or anything at all) to do with their chosen career paths.

Songs are an integral part of learning, especially in the early years of school, so why all of a sudden do we let the music fade away as kids get older? The alphabet, the days of the week, the months of the year, and even conjunctions, have been taught and made easier to learn through song. So why is music an afterthought in schools? According to the Save the Music Foundation, "More than five million public school kids don't have access to music education," which to me is insanely tragic.

Big SAM is the future of business, technology, and commerce because, unlike the other traditional academic disciplines, Big SAM requires creativity that can't be produced artificially. IBM's Watson proved that it could answer trivia questions like the ones on *Jeopardy!* and other such computers have been programmed to solve complex math problems that have concrete solutions. But what robot or computer could recreate the beautiful one-handed touchdown reception by Odell Beckham Jr. in 2015 or execute with perfection the Biles's gymnastic maneuvers that are so difficult, that Simone Biles herself is the only one who has ever done them successfully? And unless you have lived under a rock your entire life, almost everyone has bobbed their heads, clapped their hands, and/or tapped their feet to the sounds of Michael Jackson, Madonna, the Beatles, Beyonce, Elton John, and Taylor Swift. There's no way that a computer can pull off the creation of awe-inspiring artwork that takes your breath away without a human creator making it happen.

Big SAM doesn't require licensure or certifications to create opportunities and it allows for those who utilize aptitude in these areas to chart their own paths. Learning academic courses such as math can help someone get a good "job" in engineering or another math-based field, but can't necessarily be applied to their everyday lives or building money-making opportunities without other skills mixed in. People spend hundreds and thousands of dollars to hear and experience the music people have created, but I don't know a single person who would pay to watch or listen to a person rattling off math equations and their solutions—do you? If I need to know the answer to math problems I can't figure out for myself, I whip out my (free) handy-dandy calculator or look them up on Google (which is also free). No "human computer" needed (sorry, Mrs. Katherine Johnson).

CHAPTER 3
SYSTEMS R . . .

Complicated for no good reason. I believe many skool systems are best summed up in the lyrics of "Ex-Factor" by Lauryn Hill who talked about making simple things hard for no apparent reason. School systems are incredibly complex and there are so many intricacies that go into their structure, but I am going to do my best to make things simple. If we stop making things so complicated, we can greatly improve schools.

Public education systems were originally designed to formally institutionalize people in order to educate them in a way that they would be "productive citizens." However, over time, some public schools have expanded their scope to provide social services, including healthcare, counseling, substance abuse programs, and safety and violence prevention. With all of these roles placed on the shoulders of public education systems, there is no wonder why many skoolz are unable to truly meet the educational needs of young people. However, it is important to note that even with all the services provided by school systems, the methods by which kids are educated by the system should be completely overhauled. Students can have a more holistic experience that will not only prepare them for their academic and/or professional futures, but also allow them to be mentally and emotionally grounded individuals who are confident, resilient, and operating in their purpose as adults.

School systems were never designed to serve children as individuals, but instead to meet the needs of a growing industrial society. If our civilization is to successfully move from industrialism to innovation, we must help nurture the individuality of each child. Unfortunately, and especially in the aftermath of the pandemic, many school systems are doing the best they can just to maintain a sense of order and mitigate chaos. Administrators and school leaders are confused and unsure of how to handle the difficulties the pandemic has added to the complexities of schools. Teachers are frustrated and are walking out of classrooms and away from the profession altogether. Students are suffering from "Covid Slide," are in overcrowded classrooms, and have lost interest in whatever is being taught. With all of these issues facing school systems, it is much easier to work to maintain orderliness for the ease and benefit of operating than it is to focus on the best interest of the children. However, I believe that both can be achieved. I will examine some of the components that make up our school systems—standards, tests, grades, policies, and mandates—and provide suggestions for how they can be upgraded, improved, and modernized for the present and the future.

STANDARDS R . . .

Vague, unrealistic, and in some cases, irrelevant.

It seems to me that ever since the implementation of the No Child Left Behind Act, schools and school systems have been trying to develop all of these so-called "standards" for children to achieve, yet they still get left behind. At the time of this writing, forty-one states, four territories, and the Department of Defense Educational Activities (DoDEA) have adopted the common core standards and have modified them to meet the needs of their state's populations. However, very few of these standards are cut and dried and there are way too many of them for children to effectively master the skills necessary to build upon them for more advanced skills. The standards, as they are written, are not only vague and extremely generalized, but they also lack a continuum from grade to grade and concept to concept. Honestly, the standards for learning are all over the place and really don't allow for a true flow of understanding concepts.

I will use the Georgia Standards of Excellence in Math to show exactly what I mean by vague and "all over the place" with the standards. These standards, published more than many years ago (2016), have an overarching set of "Standards for Mathematical Practice," which are as follows:

1) Make sense of problems and persevere in solving them.
2) Reason abstractly and quantitatively.
3) Construct viable arguments and critique the reasoning of others.
4) Model with mathematics.
5) Use appropriate tools strategically.
6) Attend to precision.
7) Look for and make use of structure.
8) Look for and express regularity in repeated reasoning.

These are incredibly ambiguous and are really not saying much. They certainly don't point to how students will take what they learn in math and apply these concepts to their everyday lives for success. What's worse is that the standards themselves do not follow a continuum that helps kids make sense of what they are learning.

For example, first graders are first introduced to money as a base ten concept in unit five (roughly the fifth month of the first-grade school year) in standard **MGSE1.NBT.7:** *Identify dimes, and understand ten pennies can be thought of as a dime. (Use dimes as manipulatives in multiple mathematical contexts.)* The next time money is introduced is in the second grade in unit two with standard **MGSE2.MD.8:** *Solve word problems involving dollar bills, quarters, dimes, nickels, and pennies, using $ and*

¢ symbols appropriately. *Example: If you have two dimes and three pennies, how many cents do you have?*

Wait . . . what?

How is it that they have a standard where they introduce money briefly to children in the first grade (just pennies and dimes) and then have an expectation for them to be able to solve word problems involving all forms of US currency without any additional instruction in math to be able to do so? Is no one paying any attention to this? How has this been going on with no one saying anything about it? This is just one example, but there are standards sprinkled all over that are very similar to this, with no way to master fundamental concepts before requiring students to be able to perform more complex tasks.

Another issue I have with the standards is that they introduce some concepts to kids, without requiring them to know the terminology that coincides with what they have learned. Georgia Standard **MGSE1.OA.3** states: *Apply properties of operations as strategies to add and subtract. *Examples: If 8 + 3 = 11 is known, then 3 + 8 = 11 is also known. (Commutative property of addition.) To add 2 + 6 + 4, the second two numbers can be added to make a ten, so 2 + 6 + 4 = 2 + 10 = 12. (Associative property of addition.)* However, there is a footnote associated with this standard that also states: *Students need not use formal terms for these properties. Problems should be within 20.* Some of you may be thinking that it may be too much for a first grader to learn and know such "big words" and "advanced terminology," but that's where you are wrong. At this age, kids are more than excited to learn as much as they can. If you teach them the terminology at this level and continue to utilize the terminology as they continue to build on these concepts, then when they are expected to "know" the terminology (i.e., for testing purposes), it is like second nature to them. In addition, the terminology that they learn in math helps build their vocabulary across the board, which reemphasizes my point from the previous chapter—teach math and language arts together, not separately!

As a teacher, I noticed that for the purpose of standardized tests, there is an expectation for children to know the vocabulary associated with the concepts they are being taught. By the time kids reach middle school, they will need to know that 8 + 3 = 11 and 3 + 8 = 11 is an example of the commutative property of addition. However, if the vocabulary of a concept is not taught when you initially teach the concept itself, why bother to have them know the vocabulary four or five years later? If by the time they get to the sixth grade, they are supposed to know the difference between the commutative property and the associative property, why not introduce it to them when they first learn the concept, so that they actually understand it? Students shouldn't be required to regurgitate terms and vocabulary for the sake of answering questions on a test. This is the ultimate in stupidity—it just makes no sense! *Especially* since you don't *have* to know the vocabulary of the concept to *understand* the concept! This is one of the most frustrating things that schools make kids suffer through. Come on, y'all—cut the crap and either teach the vocabulary from the beginning or don't require them to know it later.

I think that from a baseline standpoint, the standards *could* be beneficial, but the way they are currently written doesn't serve to set students up for success. They should be completely rewritten in a way that is relevant and that will allow for kids to truly master their learning and be able to take on more advanced concepts as they matriculate through their educational journey. However, if no one is bringing this to the attention of those writing the standards, they will remain in their current form. Well, this is my way of sounding the alarm—WAKE UP AND CHANGE THE STANDARDS! Rewrite the standards and elevate the standards so that they can truly exemplify excellence. Only then can the standards be upheld in a way that's useful to those required to learn them.

TESTS R . . .

Testy and (in education) not our "bestie." When I was a language arts teacher, there was a huge emphasis on the need for students to do well on the Georgia Criterion-Referenced Competency Tests or CRCT. This was a statewide test designed to measure the competency levels of students in math, language arts, social studies, and science. It was required for the promotion of students to the fourth, sixth, and ninth grades and there was quite a bit of focus on kids passing these tests in order for them to be able to move on to the next grade. As a teacher, I thought that if the test was so important, then it would make sense for me to find out what the kids needed to know so that they would know what to do when it was time for them to take the tests. This prompted me to scour through our language arts curriculum to make sure that what I was teaching lined up with what they were testing. Our curriculum was one that was handed down from the district and we were required to follow it as closely as possible, with very little wiggle room for our own inputs or modifications. However, in my investigation, I noticed that something was off. I began to take inventory of the percentage of the different types of questions that would be asked on the CRCT for language arts. I learned that it was very heavy on their grammar questions, but our curriculum was not heavy on grammar at all. When I searched through our curriculum, I counted that there were only seven standards of grammar that were introduced, but there were forty-nine standards of grammar that were being tested on the CRCT.

Why? Why do skool systems treat children this way? Why in the world would they set these babies up for failure? How did they suppose that kids who haven't been taught grammar through the required curriculum would be able to miraculously answer the grammar questions on a statewide exam correctly? Despite the requirement to utilize the curriculum as-is, I did the only thing that made perfectly good sense to me—I abandoned the prescribed curriculum and started to teach grammar. Our administrator for curriculum and instruction was not happy about this. I told her that it didn't make sense for the kids to not learn concepts that 1) they did not know and 2) that they would be tested on. She told me that we had to go along with the county's curriculum mandates and if the kids didn't know it, we couldn't worry about it. Well, anyone who knows me knows that if I don't think something is right, I am going to do what I can to *make* it right! And that's what I did. I taught as much grammar as I possibly could, informing them that I was supposed to be teaching them something else, but because they needed it for the test, I was going to teach them grammar anyway. Believe it or not, the kids actually appreciated that I did. When the spring came around and they took the practice versions of the test (the test was not mandatory for seventh graders), they did well on the grammar sections. Many of the students came back and told me how glad they were that I taught them those concepts or they would not have known them.

This story is just one example of how tests are either misleading or a waste of time. Does testing really benefit students or are they really just designed so that school systems can have numerical data to rattle off and use for "accountability purposes"? Why did I have to break the "rules" and be insubordinate just for my students to get what they needed for the test? Why don't schools set children up for testing success?

For their whole lives, many children of this generation have been programmed to believe that the only reason they even go to skool is so that they can take a test. (And sadly, the education that many of these young people are receiving doesn't amount to much more than that.) Over time, with the implementation of nationwide standardized tests ingrained in public schools, children have been made to think that the only reason why any meaningful work that they are doing is to select A, B, C, or D on a test over a period of four days and wait to see if their score is adequate to advance to the next grade level. We have come to a sad state of education by reducing children's brilliance to how well they can take a test. For example, during the pandemic, there were "virtual" learning environments, but for many kids, they didn't value whatever they were supposed to be learning because they knew they wouldn't be tested on it after test mandates were lifted. The intrinsic value in learning was nonexistent and even the children themselves were asking, "Why are we even doing any of this?" Kids are incredibly perceptive, and even they knew that without being bound to a statewide test, they were "virtually" untouchable (pun intended). How have we come to such a reality?

In the state of Georgia, the test is now called the Georgia Milestones, but it's based on the same premise, in which there are high stakes associated with it. I certainly believe that it is important to gain an understanding of how much students are learning. Diagnostic tests are vital to knowing a child's baseline and a comprehensive test helps get an idea of what they have learned up to a certain point. But, requiring kids to do well on a test that is based on irrelevant and difficult-to-master standards causing stress and anxiety is unfair and should be completely revamped.

A lot of data comes from test scores, but it is important to know and understand what the testing data means. There are some schools that provide tests so teachers can have an understanding of students' strengths and weaknesses and tweak what and how they teach to best meet the needs of the students, which is the way tests *should* be used. However, parents and students sometimes have difficulty with interpreting test scores, leading to confusion about what it means for them. There are different types of tests—aptitude, achievement, ability—and many different ways of scoring these tests. Some tests take points off for wrong answers while others are not punitive for providing incorrect responses. How do you know which test is which type and how they are going to score the responses? Once the scores have been calculated, how do you interpret the results and what that means for you or your child?

Many test results will provide raw scores and then the percentiles, which is a comparative measure of how an individual, school, district, or state compares to others. If a test score report provides a percentile, that percentile is more often than not a comparison of how that individual did compared to others who took the same test at the same level. For example, if you have a score report indicating that an individual was in the eighty-seventh percentile, it means that the individual scored as good as or better than 87 percent of others who took that same test at that same grade or age level. It doesn't mean that the person is as good as 87 percent of ALL others at that level, just those who took that same test. This means that the pool of test takers must also be considered when interpreting test score percentiles and not just the score itself. These are all factors to keep in mind when considering test scores and their impact on students.

GRADES R . . .

Degrading. They are based on a teacher's evaluation of a student's performance, skill level, and yes (believe it or not) behavior. They are subjective and no matter how smart children may be, grades rest solely on the shoulders of their teachers. I hate to be the one to break it to many of you, but some students on the A–B honor roll are not really A–B students. Some of them do just enough work not to get zeroes, but they are quiet and don't cause any problems, so regardless of what they have learned, they will earn an A or B off of good behavior alone. I know this sounds bad, but it's the truth, and I've known it since high school. I did whatever work I needed to do to make "good grades" but I don't know how much I really learned in my classes. There are a few in which I really had to work hard to get my grades, but in others, sometimes the difference between an A and a B came down to whether or not I was willing to share the box of Thin Mints and Shortbreads from my volunteer work at the local Girl Scout house.

The best example I can share about the lack of validity in grades comes from my tenth-grade year in high school. From the time I was very young, I had a fascination with Spanish as a foreign language. My interest was so profound that as a third grader, my mother enrolled me into continuing education courses at our local college to take a conversational Spanish course. I was an eight-year-old in a classroom full of middle-aged people and did exceptionally well. I'm not sure if I was on my way to being completely fluent (I have been told that fluency requires a level of consistency that I wasn't exposed to), but I had a great handle on the accent, pronunciation, and vocabulary of Spanish language basics. My grandmother got sick midway through the second course and I was unable to continue, so I didn't take another Spanish class until my freshman year of high school.

During my freshman year, my high school Spanish teacher was a world-language powerhouse—fluent in Spanish, French, Italian, and Portuguese—and I *loved* being in her class. I soaked up as much knowledge of the language as I could and even participated in the multicultural festival, placing in the top three in the song and dance categories. I was convinced I would take Spanish all four years and graduate as a fluent Spanish speaker. Unfortunately, that never happened because my Spanish teacher left after my ninth-grade year. I was required to take at least two years of a foreign language in order to earn a college prep diploma, so although I dreaded the thought of having another teacher, I enrolled in Spanish II during my sophomore year. It was even more of a nightmare than I could have imagined. My new teacher didn't speak the language using a Spanish accent, could barely conjugate the verbs, and often leaned on *me* for my "expertise." I was incredibly discouraged to know how little Spanish she could teach me. I knew more than the other students in the class and, of course, had a high grade as a result. Most of the time, I would spend her class working on and/or completing assignments for my other classes and had lost my interest in Spanish altogether. My teacher would offer extra credit to my grade of one hundred—a grade that was clearly not indicative of my understanding of Spanish II.

As a teacher, I was often so overwhelmed by 130-plus students that were in my classes and the mountains of paper that accumulated (because let's be clear, there is *not* enough time in a planning period to grade papers), that I guessed some of my students' grades. I apologize to any student who may have been hurt in this process, but unfortunately, it's the reality of many schools, so it's not fair to measure a kid's subject area knowledge and understanding by the grades they make. Just because students turn in homework and complete their assignments on time doesn't mean they have an understanding of what they have learned. It's important to check in with kids to see what they really know—especially if their grades are "good." When students are failing, we are often put on "high alert" that they don't understand and/or are not making an effort to complete assignments. But when students are doing well on paper, we often assume that they know what they are supposed to, which could prove to be academically detrimental as they matriculate through school.

Grades are not a very good indicator of whether or not a student has properly learned or mastered a concept and they for darn sure can't predict whether or not a person will be successful in their future. So why do we put so much emphasis on them while kids are in skool? The saddest thing is that many kids (and yes, parents and teachers too) actually attribute their level of intelligence to their grades, GPA, and/or class rank. If you are currently a student (or if you were one of those students) who don't consider yourself smart because of your GPA, I want you to stop right now and apologize to yourself—you are *not* your grades! Stop giving power to numbers that really don't matter! Unfortunately for some and fortunately for others, they determine scholarships, college admission, and sometimes job and career opportunities. However, grades are something we have been using for years to measure classroom merit despite their less-than-meritorious origins.

An excerpt from the book, *Thom Hartmann's Complete Guide to ADHD*, goes in-depth about the earliest systems of education and how grades came into being. In this book, he describes how early man provided education through a mentoring relationship in which the student was taught the fundamentals of hunting and gathering in an individualistic and consultative method. This way of conveying information to students required an in-depth understanding of each child and the nuances that contributed to that child's ability (or inability) to learn. If a child did not understand a concept or idea completely, it was up to the teacher to adjust in order to ensure that the learning was indeed mastered, and if their methods did not work, they found ways to adjust. From the beginning of time up until 1792, learning assessments were built on personal relationships between teacher and child that required the teacher to truly get to know their students.

This was quickly and universally changed by a man who may have completely impacted education for the worse and was known as the "World's Most Famous Lazy Teacher": William Farish. This man completely upended the relationship-based method of education in which the teacher came to know his/her students on a personal level in order to most effectively present the material to be learned, all with one very simple but destructive element: grades. The story is as follows:

> William Farish was a tutor at Cambridge University in England in 1792, and, other than his single contribution to the subsequent devastation of generations of schoolchildren, is otherwise undistinguished and unknown by most people.
>
> Getting to know his students, one may suppose, was too much trouble for Farish. It meant work, interacting and participating daily with each child. It meant paying attention to their needs, to their understanding, to their styles of learning. It meant there was a limit on the number of students he could thus get to know, and therefore a limit on how much money he could earn.
>
> So Farish came up with a method of teaching which would

allow him to process more students in a shorter period of time. He invented grades. (The grading system had originated earlier in the factories, as a way of determining if the shoes, for example, made on the assembly line were "up to grade." It was used as a benchmark to determine if the workers should be paid, and if the shoes could be sold.)

- Grades did not make students smarter. In fact, they had the opposite effect: they made it harder for those children to succeed whose style of learning didn't match the didactic, auditory form of lecture-teaching Farish used.

- Grades didn't give students deeper insights into their topics of study. Instead, grades forced children to memorize by rote only those details necessary to pass the tests, without regard to true comprehension of the subject matter.

- Grades didn't encourage critical thinking or insight skills, didn't promote questioning minds. Such behaviors are useless in the graded classroom, and within a few generations were considered so irrelevant that today they're no longer listed among the goals of public education.

- Grades didn't stimulate the students, or share with them a contagious love for the subject being studied. The opposite happened, in fact, as the normative effect of grades acted as a muffling blanket to any eruptions of enthusiasm, any attempts to dig deeper into a topic, any discursions into larger significance or practical application of content.

What grades did do, however, was increase the salary of William Farish, while, at the same time, lowering his workload and reducing the hours he needed to spend in the classroom.

He no longer needed to burrow into his students' minds to know if they understood a topic: his grading system would do it for him. And it would do it just as efficiently for twenty children as it would for two hundred.

Farish brought grades to the classroom, and the transformation was both sudden and startling: a revolution as rapid and overwhelming as the Industrial Revolution from which it had sprung. Within a generation, the lecture-hall/classroom shifted from a place where one heard the occasional speech by a famous thinker to the place of ordinary daily instruction.

While grades didn't help students a bit—and, in fact, had the now well-known effect of "dumbing down" entire nations—they vastly simplified the work of teachers and schools. So they spread across Europe and to America with startling speed, arriving here in the early 1800s.

Without grades, the assembly-line classroom would not be possible. With grades, whole categories of children were discovered who didn't fit onto the conveyer belt, providing an entire new realm of employment for adults who would diagnose, treat, and remediate these newly-discovered "learning disabled" children.

Responsibility for the success of learning shifted from teachers to students: when kids failed, it was their own fault, because they obviously had a defect or disorder of some sort.

A process of sorting and discarding the misfits began (just like in the shoe factory) which, to this day, rewards the "standard" and wounds the "different."

William Farish gained, but something precious was lost to generations of students thereafter: the mentored learning experience. (Reprinted with permission from Thom Hartmann, www.thomhartmann.com.)

So, there you have it folks! One of the most widely used tools in schools today is an "innovation" that allowed a tutor to become lazy and make more money while doing it and at the same time minimize the ability to truly get to know and understand his students.

MANDATES R . . .

At the core of keeping order within systems, but at the expense of students' learning.

As you can probably guess by now, I've never been that big on following rules that don't make sense and that do more harm than good. I was that child who always needed an explanation of a rule and then I needed to determine if that explanation was good enough before I would choose to follow it. I have always been fairly strong-willed and worked around as much as I could to get my way when I wanted it. It didn't always work, but hey, as my mother taught me, "Nothing hurts a failure but a try," so I always gave it a fair shot. I will explore just a few of these policies in this section—age requirements, instructional time, certification mandates, and yes, even mandates imposed by the NCAA (which is not a school, but a *system* designed to regulate athletes in high school and college)—as examples of the types of restrictions that contribute to the dumbness existing in skoolz.

As a young child, I was incredibly "smart," at least in the traditional sense of the word, and learned how to read at the age of three. I distinctly remember being about that age when my mother was at a meeting or some other gathering with a bunch of ladies when I overheard her say, "She can read. She can read well. Let's see if we can get her to read something." There was a Charlie Brown doll sitting in a chair wearing a shirt with a message on it. I knew exactly what it said and could read it very clearly, if I had wanted to. But when my mom pointed it out and told me to read it, I froze in my tracks and it was as though the cat had my tongue. The words wouldn't come out of my mouth and it made my mother appear to be a liar, although she wasn't. I never intended to make her look bad, but I completely refused. When we left, I told her exactly what the shirt said, but just couldn't and wouldn't read them in front of those people. I had a mind of my own and always wanted to do my own thing, from the start.

AGE REQUIREMENTS

By the age of four, I could read more than the words on a doll's shirt. I could read the newspaper and always found enjoyment in learning academic concepts. My parents thought I was ready for kindergarten and attempted to get me enrolled in school early, but they were stopped in their tracks. I was too young. Although my fifth birthday was only a couple of months after the start of the school year, the *law* indicated that any child who did not turn five prior to a specific date was not allowed to enroll in kindergarten at a public school. It was set up in such a way that if a parent wanted to send their child to school earlier than legally allowed, they would have to enroll in a private school for kindergarten and remain there until second grade before they would be allowed to return to public school without retention . . . I beg your pardon!

Fast forward almost forty years later and the law has not changed as my own very intelligent and advanced five-year-old child was also denied the opportunity to attend kindergarten early simply because his birthday didn't come quite on time. It made me wonder why or how it even makes sense to prevent a young child from attending school early if he or she is ready. Especially in the case of African American males, if a child is toilet trained and shows the academic and emotional intelligence necessary to do well in school, why are they prevented from doing so?

The biggest problem I have with this mandate is that, while I understand the age mandates are in place to protect social and emotional maturity levels, many schools do not create challenging environments for children that are more academically advanced. Instead, they teach to the middle, leaving children who are not academically prepared in the dust and those who are more advanced bored out of their minds. When my youngest son was finally allowed to start kindergarten, he was forced to do the ABCs and 123s that were presented as the curricula in place for the students in his grade level. At the time, we were virtually learning and the teacher complained that he wasn't engaged. I told his teacher not only did he know his complete alphabet, but he also knew all of his numbers up to one hundred *and* his shapes and needed more challenging assignments. Her response was that until and unless he had been tested, she could not provide him with assignments more academically rigorous. Then, she told me he would still be required to do the "dumbed down" assignments, which he refused to do. Sadly, this person was my colleague and, at the time, *I* was the gifted teacher for the elementary students. Despite my knowledge and understanding of gifted children and their needs, my child's advanced needs were completely ignored. In response, I withdrew him from school and let him work on ABCMouse.com and other online learning platforms that were more aligned with his academic needs.

When I was in kindergarten (although I completely lacked the sense to take a nap during our designated nap time), I was an advanced reader and enjoyed doing "academic things." So, without prompting, I would utilize this time to work on enrichment books my parents purchased from local department stores to help enhance my love of learning. I had to lay out my cot by the door so I could get the light from the hallway and one day, one of the first-grade teachers walked by and saw me working. She asked my kindergarten teacher if I wanted to spend my naptime in her first-grade reading class. It was a no-brainer for me and of course I said yes, but it demonstrated that even more than forty years ago, there was a need to meet the demands of academically advanced students and schools were incapable of doing so without allowing students to spend time in higher grade levels.

In my opinion, allowing children to go to school early if they are ready could help prevent them from becoming bored in school and acting out with unfavorable behaviors because they are not being adequately challenged in the classroom in their later years. From birth to age five, children have the greatest capacity for learning than at any other point in their lives. A young child's ability to learn language skills, build strategies for solving problems, and their heightened sense of curiosity, provide naturally ripe circumstances for a child to excel in a formal learning environment. I feel that if we let more children with "late" birthdays (that are ready to do so) start kindergarten "early," they will be better off when they get to fourth and fifth grade because they would have built their academic foundation during a time in which they are most eager and motivated to learn.

CERTIFICATION MANDATES

When I decided to go into the field of education, I really thought I would be more suited to serve in the capacity of guidance counselor. However, I learned (at the time), I would have to teach for three years before being eligible to become a school counselor. I went through the Teach for Georgia program the summer before my first teaching job began and took the first semester off to get adjusted to being a classroom teacher. In January of that school year, I started taking classes in what evolved into the GA TAPP program and began accumulating credits toward my middle grades teaching certification, which coupled with a master's degree in education, was going to take three years to complete. I didn't mind it much, because it lined up with the three-year time frame for becoming eligible to be a guidance counselor. Besides, as long as I was working toward my certification by being actively enrolled in a licensure program, I could still work as a full-time teacher. It was the perfect plan, but I never would have predicted that the No Child Left Behind Act of 2004 (NCLB) would pull my teaching job from under me like a rug and completely alter the trajectory of my education career.

Although I wasn't the greatest teacher (I am a procrastinator by nature and many papers piled up for weeks on my desk and were only somewhat conquered through a valiant push to grade them all the two days before grades were due), I cared about my students, and wanted to learn how to become a better teacher day by day. I was eighteen months into my program when the NCLB gavel slammed down with its cruel judgment and pushed me out of the classroom because of a technicality. At the end of my second year of teaching, there came a mandate from our school district that had to disclose every teacher who was not fully certified. That included me. There were other issues that went along with that disclosure and most schools didn't want to deal with the hassle that came along with non-certified teachers, so my contract was not renewed—despite the teacher shortage. Despite the fact I had already spent two full years teaching *without* a certificate. Despite the fact I was halfway to certification and a master's degree in education. Despite my desire to continue to teach and improve along the way. There was no grandfathering in, no special considerations, nothing. Just like that, my job was taken and my quest to become certified was over (the money I was making as a teacher paid my tuition). I was devastated and felt like a failure. I was disheartened and questioned my calling, but I moved on, with hopes that maybe someday I would find my way back.

Three years later, I was able to go back and obtain my certification in middle-grades education with a focus on English/language arts and mathematics. However, I always felt I should have been able to complete what I had started since I was already "in the mix." Having to step away and then come back to the classroom later as a teacher broke my momentum and the enthusiasm I had started out with. I also felt that the rule of having certified teachers was stupid. Being certified doesn't really "qualify" a person to become a teacher. My brother has been a teacher for over twenty years and he is a dream maker for so many kids. He has helped kids go to some of the top schools in the nation—Stanford, the University of Pennsylvania, the Air Force

Academy, the University of Connecticut, Duke, and Northwestern—and he has never been certified. He has worked for the type of school that doesn't get caught up in the trivialities of an extra set of credentials just for the sake of saying they have "certified" teachers. This particular school has a 100 percent high school graduation rate and a 99 percent college acceptance rate. Most of their teachers have advanced degrees and are experts in their subject areas. By contrast, the state of Georgia, which requires "certified" teachers in their classrooms, only has an average graduation rate of 82 percent and about 60 percent of their student population enrolled in post-secondary education environments. How does this make the rationale for certification make sense?

Why are skoolz overly concerned with whether or not a person can pass a test and take a certain number of courses to determine their ability to teach in a classroom? Many education majors already go through all the coursework and student teaching requirements to be qualified to teach in the classroom, so why make them do more? I was not an education major, but if they let me teach for a whole two years, what difference would another year of being not certified (but working toward certification) make? I would argue not much, especially since I was missing content-based courses, which was not my area of weakness.

If you are a teacher or have ever been a teacher, you know there is nothing you can learn in a classroom that can fully prepare you for teaching the way on-the-job training does. Harry Wong can attempt to lay out the guidelines, but it's being in the trenches daily that fortifies the heart and soul of a teacher. Either you're built for it or you're not—there's really no in-between and a certification can't qualify it. I remember the person that was hired to serve as the lead teacher for my son's fourth-grade classroom, and within seconds, I knew that she was not the one for him. She lacked a "presence" that was needed to command his attention and provide him with the structure he needed to be successful in the classroom. I brought this concern to the attention of the assistant principal and requested that he be moved to the classroom of another teacher. Her response was that she graduated at the top of her class and was highly recommended. I was doubtful, but did my best to trust the process. Unfortunately, her ability to excel as a student did not translate to her becoming successful as a classroom teacher and within months, she was removed from the classroom.

There are certified teachers that should have never been given clearance to step foot in a school, much less teach a class. But then there are others who love children and who long to fulfill their dreams to teach, but can't seem to pass a test in order to do so. There has to be a better way to get the right people into classrooms.

The No Child Left Behind Act of 2004 was designed to create a comprehensive accountability system using data from standardized tests to determine proficiency in student learning. Instead, NCLB accomplished the opposite of what it set out to do: leave kids behind. This act was so focused on a variety of different accountability measures that it totally abandoned best practices in education that led to truly successful outcomes.

NCAA MANDATES

In a YouTube video posted on July 31, 2017, Donald "Deestroying" De La Haye announced that he had lost his full football scholarship to the University of Central Florida. Although he didn't shed tears on camera, his pain was evident. You could hear the hurt in his voice and see the shock and disbelief in his body language. This talented kicker and wide receiver who used his talents on YouTube to inspire others was faced with the difficult decision of demonetizing his channel, deleting his channel altogether, or being ruled ineligible for college football. In his heart and mind, he didn't do anything wrong. In a separate video interview, he explained that one of the videos in question is of him and his girlfriend throwing a football around on a beach. He wasn't selling autographs or taking money from rich alumni as a monetary "attaboy" for a game well-played. He was just making videos and earning money from the number of views and likes he was receiving for those videos. Nothing wrong, right? According to the NCAA at the time, not so.

Since its inception, the NCAA has worked to maintain a sense of "amateurism" with collegiate athletes by ensuring student-athletes don't get paid for their sports prowess. The idea was that "pay" for athletes would come in the form of college tuition, room and board, and books. However, no other full scholarship recipients (academic, music, performing arts) had the type of restrictions that athletes had. If a full scholarship band member wanted to go play for a gig after the game on Friday night and get paid for it, there was no rule stopping them from doing so. If someone who received a dance scholarship was cast for a national commercial, it would not be an issue. These are examples of opportunities that allowed for full scholarship musicians and performers to obtain the benefit of tuition plus build an extra cushion for their lives after college. But before NIL was allowed, student-athletes were prohibited from making any additional income related to their athletic skills and abilities. So, although full scholarship athletes could graduate without having to pay back student loans, they never got any additional benefit that would remotely compare to the income their colleges received through their athletic contributions. When I was a student-athlete, they even had a rule that if you started a business unrelated to sports, you could not use your own name, image, likeness or talents to promote your business. This, in my mind, was one of the most unfair rules in college sports. In this particular instance, De La Haye created a YouTube channel where he showed off some of his sports skills and utilized the platform for others who were aspiring to take their skills to the next level. He gained popularity, which led to the monetization of his channel, and caused the NCAA's radar to go off. After many back-and-forth interactions with his compliance office, they ruled him ineligible to play college sports and stripped his scholarship because he refused to give up his YouTube channel and the earnings he made from it.

Being a college athlete is a *full*-time job. It starts from the time you wake up in the morning and you don't clock out until your head hits the pillow at night. Morning runs, team meetings, weight training, and nutrition restrictions are all imposed upon you according to the National Letter of Intent that you sign to join this elite group of "amateur" athletes. For the length of time you are a college athlete, your body is not your own and for many of these athletes, the glory that is seen by millions on Network Television and Streaming Services eludes them. Some are walk-on athletes and others are on partial scholarship, yet they too are held to the same standards as full scholarship athletes. But, if you made money and your likeness and image or anything related to your athletic abilities were used as a way for *you* to make money and the college or the NCAA couldn't get their cut, you were considered ineligible.

I am happy the NCAA has lifted its ban on this mandate, although it came too late for Donald "Deestroying" De La Haye and so many others before him. I brought this story to the forefront because the NCAA is a system, which can be compared to skool systems and districts in their implementation of regulations that contradict their intent. If the goal is for students to go to college to increase their earning power, then why would the NCAA prevent this from happening through trivial and petty policies and regulations? According to a *BizJournal* article posted in 2018, the average full-scholarship athlete at the University of Central Florida received a little under $20,000 per academic year. The average University of Central Florida graduate earns around $48,000 per year after ten years. Despite losing his full scholarship, Donald "Deestroying" De La Haye is now "deestroying" those mediocre salaries with a whopping net worth of more than $2.2 million. Although he was able to go back and finish his degree, he didn't really *need* it (if increasing earning potential is the goal). It is estimated that his YouTube videos alone help him earn roughly $1.4 million a year. Dumb systems struck again, but De La Haye was able to outsmart the system and he struck gold as a result.

ALIDA DAVIS ABDULLAH

INSTRUCTIONAL TIME MANDATES

"Instructional Time" is a key phrase in K–12 education that really boils my blood. Do you ever wonder why children aren't getting assembly programs, field trips, and guest speakers as a part of their educational experiences? Sure, sometimes funding and resources are an issue, but they are not really an excuse—parents and others are often willing to sacrifice to give or raise money to ensure that kids get supplemental learning experiences that enhance whatever they get in their classrooms. The real culprit and true perpetrator in keeping kids away from such experiences is "Instructional Time." Instructional time is one of those "accountability" constructs that someone made up to ensure that teachers were meeting the time requirements of the many ridiculous standards that have been established in skoolz. Learning is all around us and to deprive children of deeply rich learning opportunities in exchange for "instructional time" is one of the greatest crimes against kids in the educational system.

For thirteen years, kids spend the majority of their time confined within the walls of schools and the majority of skoolz focus primarily on "instructional time." Unfortunately, instructional time doesn't always focus on the best interest of the students. It is the experience, exposure, and life lessons that not only matter most, but also have the greatest impact on children. This should be at the forefront when deciding how instructional time should be spent. Sometimes listening to a guest speaker or stopping a lesson to have difficult and or life-changing discussions are much more valuable than just learning an academic concept that was outlined in a lesson plan.

One of my former students told me that the most valuable thing he learned from me was how to think. Crazy enough, that lesson and many others I introduced in my classroom never came from a prescribed curriculum or established lesson plan. Many of those lessons came because I rebelliously "stole" from the "instructional time basket" that was supposed to be used to teach the tired, boring, irrelevant curriculum that was prescribed and instead I taught what I thought was best for them. Not what was best for the school or the district, but for the *students*. Sadly, there is too much pressure on teachers to do what they are told in order to check boxes, but are not given the autonomy to do what's most important for the people that matter most. I felt the pressure too, but I didn't let it break me. It mattered more to me that those babies were going to get instruction that would benefit their lives and their futures than to go through the school year feeling "accomplished" just because I completed a district-forced curriculum.

Administrators and systems are so worried that outside learning opportunities in the form of assemblies, guest speakers, and field experiences will cut into the classroom teaching and learning time that they will do everything in their power to severely limit them for students. The biggest issue is that these experiences can't necessarily be quantified through data. Why? Because it's difficult to put them in a neatly packaged set of numbers that document the "value" of those types of experiences to have a paper trail of "accountability." Sadly, many of the decisions that are made in schools are based on these numbers—also known as data. But as we'll explore in the next chapter, data can be deceiving, and it takes discernment to decipher it.

SYSTEMS OF MASS DESTRUCTION

Much of what has been explored in this chapter has focused on mandates that come from the larger system. However, there is no way I could bring this book to publication without addressing a system that has the power to either end or further perpetuate one of the greatest threats existing in our schools today—gun violence. My heart is compelled, but I was hoping that I wouldn't have to write this—that by the time I send this to my publisher, things would have changed—but they have not. Why?

Because some systems are incredibly difficult to dismantle. There are some that are rooted in traditions that were built by powerful and resourceful institutions and organizations. These systems have been instrumental in creating a culture in which students and teachers are in constant fear from the moment they start their commute to their schools until they are safely on their way home. They are constantly looking over their shoulders as if they are the hunted. Nervously wondering, *is my community next? Is my school next? Is my classroom next? Am I next?* It is frightening to know that the place in which children spend the majority of their time (and for some, is a safe haven) is becoming a war zone. Conversations about assault rifles, putting firearms in the hands of teachers, and active shooter drills encircle children as young as Kindergarteners and start to form trauma in the deep recesses of their minds. Minds that should be innocent; minds that should be protected; and minds that should not be subject to simultaneous construction and demolition are being permanently damaged due to trauma-informed stressors that will scar them for life.

There are forces that empower these systems—systems that ban books, but don't ban weapons of mass destruction. Systems that pump loads of money into lobbying efforts to ensure that certain rights are not treaded on are the architects of a blueprint for massacres in classrooms all over the United States. How much more blood has to be spilled for a change to come? Why do our babies and the people who care for them daily have to become casualties in battles they didn't sign up for? Why is major reform to gun control laws treated like an afterthought to these incidents? Why does it seem as though there is more care for the right to an object designed to cause death and destruction than there is for the right for our young people to live?

There are many people trying to defend guns and while I respect the right to have the freedom to carry, I respect the right for young people to be given a chance to live even more. The guns are dangerous all by themselves—they *are* the defense. But who is fighting to protect the defenseless? Our babies cannot defend themselves, so we have to fight to protect them and their lives. We cannot continue to propose and support laws that focus more on the cure (active shooter drills, teachers with guns, clear bags, bulletproof vests, etc.) than the prevention (keeping weapons of mass destruction out of the hands of dangerous perpetrators). By doing so, we begin to transform the land of the free and home of the brave into the land of the imprisoned and the home of the coward—where everyone operates by fear instead of creating policy that greatly minimizes threats to begin with.

Regardless of your political beliefs, I think we can *all* agree that:

1) Children should *never* be made to feel that they can't be safe at school
2) It doesn't require an assault rifle to protect your home or hunt game and they should only be used for military warfare
3) Teachers did not sign up to go into war, but instead to nurture young people and to help mold them into thoughtful adults that are productive citizens

I beg all lawmakers to think of your children, your grandchildren, your nieces, nephews, and the families you love when gun control is proposed and anti-gun laws are opposed, because no one is immune. These tragedies are occurring in unimaginable places—small quaint towns and even affluent suburbs, where families have been intentional about living in "low-crime" areas. Please don't harden your heart and leave these babies defenseless. It is my prayer that in those moments, rather than protecting the guns, you choose to protect the babies instead.

To those families who have dealt with this type of tragedy in any form, my heart goes out to you. My heart breaks and aches any time I hear of these horrifying events, and while we cannot change the past, I have hope that together we will use these incidents to fuel the fight for so many innocent lives that are endangered by legal systems that have protected weapons for far too long.

CHAPTER 4
DATA R . . .

The numbers that are presented by research and analysis. Economic, healthcare, government, and education systems all rely on data to make changes and improvements and to receive and allocate funding. This data comes in many forms—financial expenditures, graduation rates, and accountability measures. It's enough to make your head spin and sometimes too much to process! But what does data really tell us about schools? So many people rely on the data they read about schools to make life decisions (including moving to certain places and purchasing homes), but do they really know what the numbers are saying? Data and interpretations of data are in the eye of the beholder, and it is difficult to have a clear understanding of it without having a full understanding of all the data that is being evaluated and/or presented. On the surface, we can certainly recognize facts and figures for what they are in their quantitative state, but the real story comes from digging deeper and knowing what qualitative data is behind it. The *who* behind the data also matters. *Who* (or what entity) is working with the data and how they are using test scores, graduation rates, or some other metric to paint pictures of students?

When my youngest child was about two years old, I contemplated putting him in childcare and perhaps going back to work. We lived in Minnesota at the time and although we couldn't afford to put him in childcare full-time, I wanted to explore part-time opportunities. I went on a tour of a daycare facility and the person giving me the tour recognized I had a non-Minnesota phone number and asked where I was from. I told her I was from Georgia, but her response was not at all what I expected her to say. She said, "Oooh, I would love to move to Atlanta, but the schools are so bad." This woman, like me, was African American, living in the state of Minnesota. And while the state of Minnesota boasts some of the best schools and highest-ranking educational systems in America, it also has the greatest educational disparities between African Americans and white students in the nation. My instant response was "For whom?" Then I went on to ask, "You do know that Minnesota has the highest educational disparities in the nation for African American students, right? How can you say that the schools in Atlanta are bad when the schools in Minnesota have been failing babies like ours for years?" Needless to say, I was offended and questioned her intelligence and rationale, but having this interaction opened my eyes. It helped me understand that many people take data and statistical information at face value without considering all of the underlying factors that go into those numbers and whose best interest it is to present them. This is as ignorant and dangerous as generalizing an entire group of people based on the actions of one or a few individuals who identify with that group.

The world of data can be incredibly confusing and difficult to sort through. There are so many questions to ask: Whose data is it (who is compiling the numbers and publishing them, and what is the funding source behind it)? Why is this data being published and who benefits most from the information presented? Is there more to the numbers than what we can see on the surface? I challenge you to ask critical questions and gain a full understanding of whatever data you are exposed to, whether it is in education or any other area of importance in your life. Please don't take the numbers to heart and make life-altering decisions about a school without knowing more about it—talk with other parents and local community members to gain a more comprehensive understanding of what that school is really about. It is also important to know what your values are before making decisions about schools.

When my eldest son was two, he was going to an at-home daycare run by a wonderful woman who truly loved children. She always took great care of him and he loved going to see her every day. She told me that he befriended another child who was three and attending school. They connected well with each other because he was already in school and could communicate on a higher level than the younger, less-verbally established babies in her care. I began to wonder if maybe my son needed to go to school also. He was incredibly bright and I thought that perhaps going to a more formalized learning center would be a way for him to grow academically. I found a learning center and they were doing all the "right things" by way of learning and academic instruction. They were nice enough, but they weren't the same as his babysitter. I figured that whatever they lacked by way of the comfort and nurture of his babysitter, would be compensated for in the learning he would receive. I filled out the paperwork, told his babysitter, and was prepared to take him to the new learning center. But the day before he was supposed to start, it hit me like a brick: "Would he have the kind of care that makes him feel loved genuinely for who he is? Would he be taught and exposed to the same values and standards for character that I have? Would attending a fancy-schmancy learning center guarantee him acceptance and/or a scholarship to an Ivy League school sixteen years from now?" There were no longitudinal studies on these kids to determine if he would be at the top of his class in high school or college, so why put him there? For me, it wasn't worth the switch.

When deciding between keeping my son with his babysitter or going with a learning center, I realized I valued the *care* he was receiving in his at-home daycare environment more than I valued the potential for learning he could get in the educational center. The same should hold true when looking at data and statistical numbers. Certainly, the numbers may be straightforward, but it is always important to know how the data is speaking to *you*. What are *your* values and how do these numbers play a role in what's most important in your life? When looking at data, gain an understanding of what the numbers are saying as well as what they are not saying. Sometimes data exposes the values of an institution and can help you discern if those values line up with your own, especially when funding is concerned.

In 2018, the state of Georgia spent an average of $24,070 per inmate, whereas the total cost per pupil was roughly $9,100. Sadly, the state only contributes roughly $2,600 per student, with the remainder of per-pupil funding coming from county, city, and/or district funds. The total state funding per student is almost ten times less than the amount of money spent on incarcerated individuals. There is often talk of a school-to-prison pipeline and when I see these figures, it is crystal clear why this "pipeline" exists. Anytime I have ever heard those who have been imprisoned talk to young people, they have always encouraged them to stay in school and get their "lesson." The irony in this admonishment is nauseating: a state spends more money to detain people in correctional facilities than they do to help fund schools so that fewer people end up in jail. Frederick Douglass has been known for his quote, "It is easier to build strong children, than it is to repair broken men." Yet, instead of spending the resources and energy to ensure children have what they need to be strong, the state government chooses to pour twice as much money into repairing the men that systems have broken. The result: inmates instead of innovators. This is a sad and heartbreaking truth that needs to be corrected.

Although funding numbers can be a clear indication of a system's priorities, test scores, graduation rates, and school rankings, they can be very deceptive. This goes back to values and what you feel is most important for your child. It is important for kids to get a good quality education, but what if that education is greatly impaired by their learning environment? A place can be absolutely beautiful—a high-tech, pristine building with all the bells and whistles and a curriculum designed to set children on a path to educational success, but if the environment is not conducive for your child or the way they learn, they will not achieve the success the school may boast for other kids. Does the school value diversity? Is your child the only (Black, white, LGBTQ, disabled, special needs, gifted—or some other fill-in-the-blank criteria) in their class or school? Are they a hands-on learner who would thrive in a project-based learning environment, but is in a school that primarily teaches in a Socratic method? I have known people who have moved into certain areas of town and spent an exorbitant amount of money on their homes only to discover that their child or children are miserable in the "great school" they enrolled them into. What are your values? What is most important to you? The pandemic (along with the millions of courses that exist online) has shown that you can learn anything anywhere from anyone, but your child's educational experience is often one that can't be determined by numbers alone.

I graduated from a high school rooted in pride—graduating alongside some incredibly talented and successful people who are doctors, NFL athletes, college coaches, mental health professionals, attorneys, teachers, and entrepreneurs. But based on numbers alone, the statistics painted us as one of the worst schools in the city. If you only looked at our graduation rate and national test scores, you might think we were all doomed for failure. We didn't have all the state-of-the-art facilities and resources some other schools had (many of our classes were held in an old elementary school building and our track was made of cinder), but we made the best of what we had. We may have gone through things at our school that students at other schools didn't (my high school experience was a lot like the movie, *Lean on Me*, featuring Morgan Freeman), but all schools have their own share of issues and problems. We had our fair share of hardships, but we were able to overcome the challenges we faced—we were confident, resilient, and ambitious. There are so many successful graduates who have come out of my high school and are thriving. Numbers and statistical information painted a grim picture of my high school at the time and its reputation in my hometown was poor. However, a person's trajectory in life can't just be based on numerical data and statistical information. Regardless of what the numbers may have said, no statistical figure could have predicted the numerous success stories that came from the "School on Da Hill."

When assessing statistical data, whether it's referring to schools, the healthcare system, government, employment and labor, or economic entities, it is important to take the funding source, intended purposes, and desired outcomes of that data into consideration before making major life decisions based on those numbers. Many private organizations and corporations conduct research and studies for the purpose of promoting a concept or product that will generate revenue for themselves and/or their stakeholders. Pharmaceutical companies tout the effectiveness of a particular drug in clinical trials, especially in the early stages when generic versions of the drug cannot be created. Political studies and research will often present findings that increase society's trust and confidence in the government. The numbers and statistical figures may be factual, but it is always important to gain a deeper understanding of the context of this data and how it translates to your own personal needs and values.

There is much to be said about the qualitative data that doesn't show up in written documents. Have you ever walked into a place and it just *felt* right? Energy is contagious and it is a powerful force that can speak to your inner being in many ways if you are open to hearing its voice. No matter what the numbers say or how others may judge a place, only *you* know if a place is right for you. If you are seeking a new school for your children, a new place for your family, or a new job for yourself, the data you gather from just going there and observing is just as valuable (if not more valuable) as reading statistical data about the place. By going to a location and experiencing it firsthand, you are able to obtain information that numbers alone cannot provide. You are able to see how teachers and students interact with one another and feel the "vibe." Oftentimes, you will know within the first few moments and in your initial interactions with administrators, teachers, and students whether it is a good fit for your children and your family. Don't disregard those feelings—they play a role in determining what's right for you and establishing the criteria for what serves you and your family best.

I have had the distinct privilege of visiting some top schools across the nation. Two of them that stuck out to me were the Marcus Garvey School in Chicago, Illinois, and Roses in Concrete in Oakland, California. If I were to have only considered the published statistical data for the year I visited, I may have missed how amazing these schools were. According to the data for 2017, the Marcus Garvey School published that only 22.5 percent of their student population was prepared for the next grade level (which was likely based primarily on standardized test scores). A 22.5 percent readiness rate is dismal. However, the school was anything but. It was alive—overflowing with love, nurture, and a desire to learn. It was data that couldn't be defined using the established parameters of the state's report card . . . What I experienced during my visit was a stark contrast to what the numbers demonstrated. I saw something totally different—a sense of pride, belonging, and excellence greeted me from the moment I stepped into the building. A young man with curly hair and a bright smile led the group and welcomed me and my colleagues into their school. The young people conducted a tour of the school, which felt a lot like home. Each teacher had their door decorated with the colors and mascots of their alma maters and the walls were vibrant and displayed artwork and academic works of excellence. The tour culminated in a classroom observation that was interactive and inclusive. The students showed us what they were learning and the methods by which they were taught and it was impressive. A variety of learning styles were implemented to meet the needs of the multiple intelligences that each individual student possessed. Despite the numerical data that was published about the school, this was a stellar learning environment in which administrators established high standards, teachers cared, and students were thriving.

I learned about the Roses in Concrete school just a few months prior to my trip to Oakland. Founded by Jeff Duncan-Andrade, I recall him doing a presentation about the school at an event for Educators 4 Excellence during their annual teacher's conference and retreat. His presentation, entitled "Note to Educators: Hope Required When Growing Roses in Concrete" left me intrigued and mesmerized. The students were the roses and he described the concrete as physical violence and PTSD, racism, gentrification, poverty, patriarchy, institutional violence, and educational and economic apartheid. These were the grounds from which these roses were growing and they needed hope to grow. He talked about the history of Roses in Concrete school and how they got permission from the elders and indigenous locals to start the school, their urban garden which serves as a food supply for the community, and how they got clearance from Tupac Shakur's mother, Afeni Shakur, to name the school after his famous poem. Dr. Duncan-Andrade shared the dire circumstances from which many of the students come and how they thrive at his school in spite of those backgrounds. As he spoke, I imagined this school as a "magical place" that was a refuge for children in a neighborhood that was torn with crime, poverty, and instability for many of its students. His talk laid out all of the numbers—poverty and crime rates, along with the education disparities and low test scores of the students in his school's community versus surrounding areas. However, as dire as the numbers and circumstances of these students may have seemed, I knew that Roses in Concrete was a special place and that those connected to it couldn't be defined by the statistics surrounding it. At the end of Jeff Duncan-Andrade's presentation, I still wanted to hear more and to learn more about their methods and approaches to education and their effectiveness for the community it served.

A few months later, I got the opportunity to see and experience it for myself and I was blown away. We went into a dual-language immersion kindergarten classroom where half of the day was taught in Spanish and the other half in English to accommodate the Spanish-speaking students learning English and to bridge the communication gap between their English-speaking classmates. In this same classroom, five- and six-year-olds learned about how butterflies' migration could be compared to how some immigrants from Mexico migrated to the United States. I met fourth graders who were in the process of writing letters of affirmation to children who were caught up in a slave trade in chocolate factories. We traveled to the art studio where we saw the beautiful costumes designed by students for their spring theater production. Every year, they selected a traditional play and rewrote it to address a social justice issue that was prevalent during that time. The fifth graders' "Senior Thesis" addressed the Trayvon Martin tragedy and how that situation could have been different. All throughout the school were parent and community volunteers committed to giving the school their all. It wasn't a brand-new building, and although the facilities/resources may not have been state-of-the-art, the learning was progressive and was far more advanced than I had seen in some schools with greater resources. As we walked out of the building, I gave one of the school's volunteers a big hug and whispered "thank you" to her through my choked-up voice. When I got back on the bus to debrief about our visit, my heart was overflowing with emotion and tears streamed uncontrollably down my face. I was in disbelief. I couldn't believe that a school filled with students who faced so many challenges could have such an amazing educational experience and it wasn't about the numbers. That school year, only 17 percent of their student population met or exceeded proficiency in ELA and 7 percent in math for the California Assessment for Student Performance and Progress (CAASPP). While these numbers could be seen as dreadful, they didn't tell the whole story of the students or the school. Were the kids learning? Absolutely! Unfortunately, those standardized test scores could only capture the responses from a test, but not the depth of compassion, resilience, and sense of community that was being taught on a daily basis. There was love and nurture permeating all over, in, and throughout that place and although it has been many years since I visited, it still gives me chills and my heart is filled with joy from the memory.

At an education event hosted by the Bush Foundation in Minnesota, I attended a session in which I learned about the graduation rates for the High School for Recording Arts (HSRA), which for the previous year was 31 percent. This was in stark contrast to the 82.5 percent statewide graduation rate for other public schools in the state, but I knew that those numbers weren't telling the whole story. I had always heard great things and some amazing success stories about the High School for Recording Arts, so I knew there was much more to the story than what those statistics expressed. I had the good fortune of being in the same space as the school's executive director, and thought it was the perfect opportunity to learn more. I asked him what those graduation rates meant and why they were being celebrated despite being much lower than the state average. He explained to me that HSRA, at that time, had the highest graduation rate nationally for a school of its kind. Similar to what may be known in other communities as a "reform school" or "alternative school," I learned that HSRA has been able to successfully graduate students who are or who have been homeless, teenage parents, incarcerated, runaways, and dropouts. Many schools nationwide and in the state with similar populations did not share this same level of success. It is a school where young people who have been written off and discarded by other schools and sometimes even by their own families can find their voice—both literally and figuratively.

Unfortunately, statewide school report cards are only capable of publishing numbers, percentages, and statistics about schools because they are easy to obtain and analyze. School data and reporting can be streamlined using colorful charts and fancy-looking graphs to display their "findings." However, data is everywhere and all around us at all times and our whole beings are data centers. We don't need calculators, spreadsheets, and software programs to analyze whether what we are experiencing aligns with our values and meets the standards we have established for ourselves and our children. Although we sometimes dismiss it, children are even better at analyzing nonnumerical data than adults. When determining the right fit for a child, it is very important for them to be a part of the process as well because they are able to evaluate what they are seeing and feeling through the lens of what they will experience for themselves while parents will be away from the school during the day—in their homes, on their jobs, and/or working their businesses.

In retrospect, I missed out on the opportunity to attend a college and select a major that was much more aligned with my own passions, interests, and talents, because I valued external sources of quantitative data and ignored what the qualitative data of my own intuition was trying to tell me. When I was a junior in high school, I worked briefly at a store called "Merry Go Round" in our local mall. My assistant manager's brother came in and we were having a conversation about what I wanted to do when I graduated and where I wanted to go to college. At the time, I was set on majoring in premed and becoming a neurosurgeon, but with just a few words, he completely helped change my career trajectory—and my life. He knew I was a student in a math-science-technology magnet at my high school and in that conversation, he told me, "You should become a chemical engineer." To be honest, I didn't really know what an engineer was but, intrigued, I continued to listen. "Chemical Engineers make $50,000 (which at that time was a lot of money) when they graduate from college. You could become a chemical engineer and even if you don't end up in medical school, you will still have a career and make lots of money instead of just majoring in premed." So, at that moment, with those large monetary figures at the forefront of my mind, I decided I would go to school for engineering. I shared this information with my science teacher, who encouraged me to apply for the Minority Introduction to Engineering (MITE) program. I applied for the programs at both Tuskegee University and Auburn University in Alabama. It was at the Tuskegee University MITE program where I met a young man who would eventually become my husband. But neither of us became engineers. Because of the impressive numbers and all the data surrounding it, I chose one of the top STEAM schools in the nation to pursue engineering. But over time, I learned that I was not motivated by the dollar signs that initially attracted me to the field of engineering, and the quantitative data that impressed me so much in the beginning, left me miserable and trying to figure out my life's work once I finally graduated.

THE MYTHICAL "PERMANENT" RECORD

In the grand scheme of things, macro data about entire schools and systems is very well preserved and archived, but individual contributions to those numbers are lost. A lot of focus is given to the big numbers—attendance rates, graduation rates, GPAs, and test scores. However, the individual records of students are rarely kept, especially after long periods of time. From a research perspective, if a longitudinal study were to be done to determine the effects of educational practices or local/national/world events on students during a particular time frame, this data would be difficult (if not impossible) to obtain. From a personal standpoint, if you just wanted to know what your national test scores or grades were in the third grade, they are likely nowhere to be found. How is it that individuals' personal data and information are used in a variety of different ways, but the individual is unable to obtain and/or utilize that data for themselves? This is the myth of the "Permanent Record."

Many schools have not done a great job of keeping individual records for students and their parents. Regardless of what state and/or school district you grew up in, it is probably very difficult to find your "permanent record," and if you do, it may not even consist of your grades, attendance, discipline/behavior, and test scores. It's possible that it will only show that you were a student, and when you were a student, and if you graduated—nothing more, nothing less. If you went to school prior to digital databases, you may not be able to access your school records at all.

Right before I started teaching K–5 gifted students, I really wanted to know what my gifted scores were and what areas kept me out of a program I desired so desperately to be a part of. I made a phone call to the school district where I spent all thirteen of my formative education years. I stayed at the same elementary school from kindergarten to sixth grade, went to the same junior high school in both the seventh and eighth grades, and graduated from the same high school I started out in, with no changes to other schools. Yet, when I called to find out how to get a hold of my "permanent record," I learned they didn't have one for me. I was told it was likely destroyed because it had been so long since I was in school. I was confused, disappointed, and felt completely deceived by the system. The idea of a "permanent record" has been used for years over the heads of children, shaking in their boots with worry over the opportunities they may be denied if something bad was in it—but it doesn't even exist. When I started a position that required me to obtain transcripts and academic records for students, I learned that in some places, they don't keep records for even a short time after you graduate. They have a way to tell whether or not you graduated, but other than that, none of your file actually exists. (*On a side note, parents who need this data to change schools sometimes have difficulty retrieving it. Many school districts, especially in places where there are assigned schools, require families to provide social security cards, birth certificates, rental agreements/mortgage documents, and even utility bills just to enroll. They may also require families to provide transcripts and/or grades from the school(s) their children are coming from. All of these documents are the personal property of the family, yet when they request those documents to change schools, unnecessary obstacles are in place to prevent or greatly hinder their retrieval. Making families jump through hula-hoops just to get a hold of documents that already belong to them is unfair, inconvenient, and downright dumb. This should not be!*)

This is the perfect example of the lack of importance of the individual to the school and/or school district. Systems will make use of the numbers that a child contributed to the test scores, graduation rates, attendance numbers, and whatever other metrics are being used to measure school climate and performance. However, once that child leaves the system or graduates, it's almost as if he/she/they never existed in that system. So how much do these numbers really matter in the grand scheme of things? These numbers don't determine how successful or how much of a failure a person will become, so why do we give them so much credit? If a person graduates at the top of their class, it is nice to ooh and ahh about it, but it doesn't define who they are or determine what they will be in life. I have known people who were not even in the top 10, 20, or 50 percent of their graduating class thriving and living their "best lives" and the numbers had nothing to do with it. This whole chapter has been dedicated to the hope that none of us let quantitative statistics define who we are or make us feel "better than" or "inadequate." Perhaps you are a divorcee, single parent, or qualify/qualified for free and reduced lunch as a student, but those numbers alone don't tell the whole story of who you are—no number can do that and it's important we recognize we are all much more than whatever statistical numbers have been used to label us.

PART II
PEOPLE R . . .

So now that we know:

Pandemics R unprecedented and wreak havoc on our lives, especially for children, and there is no way we can go back to business as usual;

Curricula R ridicula and often don't provide learning content or methods that build young people up for successful futures;

Systems R designed to establish a baseline that allows for the efficient and orderly administration and teaching for the masses; and,

Data R pieces of information that mean nothing without the stories that go with them.

These concepts have set the foundation of what's next—the nitty-gritty of this book. Allow me to reemphasize that much of what is being written is based on my own experiences, thoughts, and beliefs. I won't be citing formal studies and research because many of these are just examples based on what I have either witnessed, endured, or thought about. Certainly, there may be studies on similar situations and maybe as you read these pages, you can relate to some of the stories and the people they are based on. However, the premise of this section is simple: the power is in the people. This section is designed to highlight the importance of the people within the schools—not a school's name, reputation, or recognition, and certainly not the rigor of a curriculum or the raving statistics that it may boast. Without the people, the schools are nothing and they don't exist. The pandemic helped to prove this fact, and unfortunately, many of us are experiencing this the hard way.

Let's explore how the people have the ability and the power to reverse the (stupidity) of skoolz and help our current and future generations operate with the power of knowing that schools can't define them, determine their future, or decrease and increase their value.

Skoolz R Dumb. People R Powerful. People R Smart. People make or break schools, and we must outsmart the system by dismantling the idea that it's the other way around.

CHAPTER 5
ADMINISTRATORS R . . .

Responsible for setting the tone. Whether it's the superintendent, the executive director, or the principal of a school, it is an administrator's vision, mannerisms, and leadership style that establishes the environment of what makes a school successful or not so successful. Teacher and staff satisfaction, and in many cases, performance, rests on the shoulders of administrators. As the conductor of an educational environment, administrators make the difference between a faculty that works together to create harmonious melodies and a teaching staff that is a messy mash-up of screeching and clanging. People want to be treated well, feel a sense of work-life balance, and be appreciated, regardless of the profession. Institutions that possess these qualities are led by concertmasters who create beautiful symphonies within their organizations. However, if you show me a school where there is a lot of teacher turnover, I will show you a cacophonous skool with a tone-deaf leader who is difficult and unwavering. The field of education is already one in which people give so much more of themselves than what they often get back (especially financially), so if teachers are quitting at a record pace, you can almost always point back to leadership. How well do administrators support their teachers in difficult situations? How much extra work do administrators require beyond what teachers are already expected to do with little or no appreciation? Are administrators flexible when teachers have personal issues related to their families? Are school leaders even aware that they are often the reason why some teachers leave? Probably not, but I wish they were.

Most educators consider themselves lifelong learners and although many enjoy the reading and researching aspect of learning—some of the best lessons don't come from journals, projects, papers, or lectures. It comes in the form of constructive criticism and learning from mistakes. Knowing this, wouldn't it be great if structures were in place to require administrators to obtain open and honest feedback from those who serve under their leadership as a form of professional development? Unfortunately, it is not always easy to receive criticism from the bottom up. Behind closed doors, with their friends, and in the pages of private journals, teachers express their anger, hurt, frustration, and disappointment about administrators and those in leadership. The dissatisfaction they feel sometimes festers inside until they find themselves in a hostile work environment that leads to them either resigning from their positions or leaving the field of education altogether. These teachers are torn, knowing they have to leave behind the students they love so dearly in order to maintain their own peace and sanity. I, too, have found myself in this position and wondered to myself: how many teachers actually express these feelings to their administrative leaders? How many are concerned that sharing their frustrations will actually cause more harm than good or be a waste of their time? How many administrators can accept the truth from their constituents and use it to help them become better leaders?

In the spirit of professionalism and a desire to prevent burning bridges, many people will not openly admit that it was the administration that caused them to jump ship. You may hear things like, "I was stressed out," "I needed to make more money," or "I got a better opportunity," but very rarely will people come out and tell the truth about why they left a teaching position or the field of education. I tend to be the kind of person who speaks the truth—good, bad, or ugly—but even I have bitten my tongue about the real reason why I had to resign from some of my previous teaching (and administrative) positions. Many teachers feel it's not a battle worth fighting, especially if they have endured a number of headaches prior to finally submitting their notice. But what if there was a way for teachers to share their grievances about their experiences without fear of retaliation in the form of bad recommendation letters or being blackballed amongst other educators? What if they could give their administrators a piece of their minds (in the form of "professional development") through their grievances without worrying about backlash?

I've been on both sides. I used to serve in an administrative role, so I know how stressful the job can be. There are difficult, split-second decisions that have to be made on a regular basis, and administrators are often caught in the middle between higher powers (and their infinite demands) and the needs of their teachers. Administrators have a very tough job! Many administrators come from the classroom, but when they come into leadership it's important for them to define their role; crafting it with the same care and sense of connection they had when they were teaching, and not allow the title to define them. Sometimes it's easy to forget what it was like as a teacher when the pressures of leadership are choking the life out of those who are serving in administrative roles. Sometimes it's easier for teachers to bite their tongues and walk out the door than it is for them to bite the bullet and tell an administrator how they really feel. For the teachers who have bitten their tongues, holding back how they really feel, and for the administrators who want to be empowered to elevate their leadership skills through real life examples, this chapter is for you.

Leadership is about more than just holding a title or having the credentials that qualify someone to serve in a supervisory position. It is about building relationships and making connections with those you will be working with in order to achieve a collective goal. I have been a witness to schools where administrators provide autonomy to teachers, trust in their professionalism, and solicit honest feedback without judgment and backlash. They are thriving hubs, where teacher morale is high and teacher turnover is low. It is the type of leadership that is rooted in empathy and humanity that walks a fine line between holding teachers to a high standard while providing them the support necessary to be their best selves in the classroom, and beyond. I have also experienced ineffective leadership that has led to a domino turnover effect, with good teachers leaving behind kids who so desperately need them because the "grown-folks" don't know how to act. This is a heartbreaking reality that I hope to address. There is a popular cliché phrase that says, "Knowledge is power," and I have dealt with some difficult and uncomfortable situations that have led to the "knowledge" I am sharing in this chapter.

In the following pages, I hope to provide some insights into how leading with care has the power to completely revolutionize the working environment for teachers and the learning experience of students. If you are ready and can handle the power in these truths, this is my "Power Points and Pain Points Guide for Administrators."

PAIN POINT: NOT TREATING INDIVIDUAL CIRCUMSTANCES DIFFERENTLY—ESPECIALLY IN A PANDEMIC (OR OTHER DIFFICULT AND UNPRECEDENTED SITUATIONS)

Covid-19 taught us all many lessons, and one of them is that no two people are alike. It is a virus that operates asymptomatically in some and has proven to be fatal in others. With that in mind, there is no way that leaders should continue to approach how they lead individuals with a generalized mindset. We are in a time in our history when overall "tough love" leadership is ineffective—people need more than an iron fist to motivate teams. At the same time, we must have high expectations of ourselves and others to be and to do our very best. One of the best ways to balance high expectations and standards is with grace and understanding. After the nation went on the initial quarantined lockdown that lasted much longer than anyone would have expected or wanted, it was my hope that Covid-19 would have at least allowed for those in charge to give their subordinates grace, but in many cases, it only made them more rigid. All across the country, there were unrealistic and unfair demands being placed on teachers. Some administrators had an expectation that teachers should show up without complaint and put their lives on the line.

Unfortunately, my situation was no different . . .

After the shutdown of the spring and the summer months stuck at home with drive-by modifications of milestone celebrations and kids playing in sprinklers because all the pools were closed, there was still much uncertainty at the start of the school year in the fall of 2020. I had been assigned a new position teaching elementary school talented and gifted students that previous spring, prior to the lockdown, so it was going to be uncertain for me anyway. I reached out to my new administrative team to get an idea of their expectations of me and to gain an understanding of what I needed to prepare for in my new role, but I never got a reply. I was apprehensive because I had always worked with middle school students, so I wasn't sure about working with a much younger student population. Nevertheless, I was excited and wanted to make sure I was prepared for them in the fall. Despite my many attempts to connect with my new principal, I never got a response to my emails, so I proceeded through the summer with the understanding that I would find out more as we got closer to the start of the year.

In addition to trying to get information about my expectations as a new teacher in an elementary environment, I needed to find out more about their teaching expectations in the midst of the pandemic so I could figure out how to navigate my role as a mother to four children who would also be engaged in virtual learning. My oldest son had already been accepted to an independent school that would start the year in a hybrid style and my daughter (who was starting the first year of middle school) and youngest son (who was a rising kindergartner) would be attending the K–8 charter school where I was working. My youngest daughter was still enrolled in her district-assigned neighborhood school, and once I learned they would be learning virtually, I figured it wouldn't matter because we would all be at home anyway. Without any guidance from the school where I was working about how they wanted me to approach teaching and learning, I shifted my focus to making sure I properly prepared my own children for their school year in this "new normal." I set up a space in our home complete with desks and each child had their own cubby with their own school supplies. We established specific places they could go if they needed to be able to focus without the noise and distractions of their siblings' classes. I had a space for myself in a nearby room to be able to teach my classes without distractions, but yet, close enough to the kids to keep an ear and eye out if they needed me. I was ready, and for the first time, I was actually organized. I even agreed to work with one of my daughters' friends who would be in the same classes so that her mom could work at her job while I helped all the kids. Everything was set, and I was optimistic about making the best of a pretty horrible situation.

I finally got to the first days of preplanning and I was excited to get out of the house and actually see some of my colleagues and just be able to connect with humans outside of my home and neighborhood. It had only been a few months but seemed like a lifetime since we were able to occupy the same space with people other than those in our households. Wearing masks and finding ways to physically distance ourselves, we were happy to be back together again. In that one large assembly meeting with both the elementary and the middle-level teachers in attendance, we listened to the plan for our return, and I quickly learned that their so-called "plan" would cause everything in *my* plan to come crumbling down. They wanted teachers to come into the building every other week, which I thought was pretty strange and (actually quite ridiculous since we had spent the last eight weeks of the previous school year teaching from home). I couldn't figure out how teaching from a classroom (especially if you had children of your own) would be safer and/or more effective than being at home if you were going to be on Zoom (or Google Hangouts, or Microsoft Teams) anyway.

Like me, many teachers had already established some sort of home-classroom environment as a result of the lockdown and were prepared (and looking forward) to teach from home. However, others felt that they needed to be in their actual classrooms in the building to have more focus on teaching and felt that they would perform more effectively in this setting. Perhaps they needed/wanted the consistency of the classroom arrangement and tools. But when they were in their off week and went back home, they would have to "make do" until it was their turn to be back on campus. With these varying needs in mind, I felt that it would have made sense to get a better understanding of each teacher's individual needs so that they could establish their own sense of consistency for their classes instead of having teachers flip-flop back and forth between home and school. Why not let those teachers who needed and/or wanted to come to the building serve in their classrooms and allow those with extenuating circumstances, or had people in their homes with compromised immunity, or who were just uncomfortable about Covid, work from home? That way, teachers working in the building could establish their classrooms in a way that worked best for them and those working from home would be able to manage their personal and work lives in a way that created a sense of balance.

I expressed my concern about the plan for us to come into the building every other week instead of just working from home and coming into the building on an as-needed basis. From one assistant principal, I was told that they don't have any power to change or modify this plan. The other assistant principal was trying to convince me that we were in a better situation than many other schools. He would talk about how we should be grateful to have our jobs because other teachers were losing theirs, and I was definitely grateful. However, I couldn't believe how inflexible they were being in a time like this, and I pleaded with them to consider my circumstances and work with me to make it a better situation for everyone involved. I think their idea was to have a hybrid strategy in which everybody had to make a sacrifice for "accountability" purposes, but why create an unnecessary sacrifice just for the sake of doing so?

Despite my protests insisting this made no sense in my situation, they assured me that it would work. Their plan for my situation was for me to come into the building every other week and (were *allowing* me to) bring my kids with me to the classroom. Even this was stupid and potentially dangerous, as every public building had to be outfitted with a sign that said, BY ENTERING THE BUILDING, I ACCEPTED THE POTENTIAL RISK OF THE EXPOSURE TO COVID-19. I didn't want this for myself, and certainly not for my children, but leaving them at home without supervision for their school day was not an option. As a "consolation prize," they told me I could bring blankets for my kids to be "comfortable" (to lie all over the cold linoleum floors) and were giving me "special clearance" to get a refrigerator and microwave to set it up in my classroom. They literally recommended I bring and set up a microwave, small refrigerator, and blankets for my kids on Monday and take that stuff back home on Friday, work from home for a week, and then bring it all back the following week. On top of all that, they wanted me to bring all four of my kids (plus my daughter's friend, who is immunocompromised) into one classroom as I taught my classes all day. At the time, they were all doing remote learning in kindergarten, fourth, sixth, and eighth grades. If I left the room to have a quiet space for me to teach, they were unsupervised (and if they needed to go to the restroom, they had to be monitored and walked there), but if I remained, it was a noisy hot mess for everyone. At home, everyone had a designated space, had access to the toilet without needing an escort, and could have a snack at their designated break times without having to interrupt my teaching if their times didn't coincide with mine. I couldn't figure out how they were making sense of it and how they expected me to teach effectively with this arrangement.

It was taking a toll on my physical and mental health and well-being, and I knew it was only a matter of time before I would have to find another position, despite the fact that "other schools were firing teachers" and that I "should have been grateful to have my job because other places weren't hiring" (according to them). I believe in a higher power that already had it worked out and in the midst of all that, I *was* blessed with another opportunity. When I submitted my resignation, there was no "exit interview" for me to provide feedback and the principal sent a one-word response to my email: "Okay."

In that moment, administrators had the power and unique opportunity to lead with compassion and implement a *real* strategy including input from the people it affected most. Instead, their rigidity led to more frustration. This was not the time for dictatorial leadership, but one in which administrators needed to find a way to provide support for teachers and minimize the individual barriers to effective teaching—not create *more* obstacles during an already stressful time. A simple solution would have been to survey all teachers and find out what worked best for them and why. From there, they could have implemented a *real* strategy that contained input from the people it affected most. I can't speak for other teachers, but if the administrators I was working with at the time had helped to accommodate my individual circumstances, it would have shown me that I was a valued member of the community and provided the support I needed to help me bring my best self to my students.

POWER POINT: BUILD RELATIONSHIPS WITH YOUR TEACHERS AND DIRECT REPORTS FROM THE VERY BEGINNING

I believe that much of the frustration that took place when trying to have the opportunity to work from home came directly from a lack of understanding, all because my school leader refused to get to know me from the beginning. Unlike many teachers who go through the traditional application-to-interview-to-hiring process, I was appointed to the position and didn't have the opportunity to connect with my new school leader beforehand. Because of this, it was important for me to learn more about her vision and leadership style, and gain an understanding of her expectations. As soon as I learned of my new assignment as a teacher under her leadership, I sent the principal an email to let her know I wanted to meet with her so we could get better acquainted and gain a mutual understanding of one another. As a new person on her staff, I felt these were vital elements in building a good relationship and doing my job successfully. However, she never responded to my initial email or to the many subsequent attempts to reach her. The school year was about to begin and my requests to have a "get to know you" meeting were denied and deferred to her assistant principals.

Unfortunately, I was unable to get to know this administrator, and she had no idea about my background, teaching philosophies, or educational outlook (and I knew nothing about hers either), all because she refused to meet with me. My new role was part-teaching and part-administrative in nature and involved testing, data management, and teaching. I felt slighted by my unanswered emails and completely baffled that she would not prioritize getting to know me better and learning how my personality and skillset would fit into the already established culture.

Sadly, the only meeting I actually had with her was centered around my objection to the week-on, week-off teaching plan. In this meeting, she said, "I *know* my staff, so I had to make a decision that was right for the entire faculty." I was truly disappointed by this statement because she never took the time to get to know *me* and I hate that we missed the opportunity for us to gain an understanding of one another prior to dealing with a situation that escalated into a meeting about my grievances for the school's pandemic teaching plan. If a new person joins your team, they shouldn't have to chase you down to learn about your vision or to find out the norms of the organization. I believe that if we had gained an understanding of each other from the start, then the issue could have been resolved much more easily, or perhaps it may not have been an issue at all.

It is important to the entire organization that the leader (whether it is a coach, teacher, or school principal) connect with his or her constituents from the very beginning to get a feel for who they are and how their strengths and abilities will fit into the overall strategy/vision/plans of the organization, classroom, or team. This is also the best chance to establish a strong working relationship by outlining your expectations as a leader from the start. Reach out to them from the beginning, even if just for a short moment to introduce yourself and for them to get to know who you are. By knowing up front who you are and how you operate, subordinates know your expectations and standards and what they need to do to meet and/or exceed them. You can't just show up out of the blue and expect your constituents to do whatever you tell them to without having an understanding of your vision and how they fit into it. People don't operate well like that.

POWER POINT: EFFECTIVELY COMMUNICATE LEADERSHIP CHANGES WHEN THEY OCCUR

Just as a new person to an organization shouldn't have to go out of their way to seek out those in leadership positions to find out their first steps, if you are a new leader in an already established environment, your employees, athletes, or students shouldn't have to find out by chance that you are the new person in charge. Leadership changes can be difficult and the best way to facilitate a shift in command is through clear communication.

Collegiate athletes, past and present, know the amount of stress and pressure that goes into the recruitment process and the need to perform in order to achieve the goal of a scholarship offer. The coaching staff and your future teammates are just as important (if not more important) as the school itself in making the decision to commit to participating in sports at the college level. I had been recruited for months by the college that was at the top of my list and had already been offered a partial scholarship in track and field. Although I had already signed my National Letter of Intent, my future college head coach came to my last region track meet to see me run. I was excited and looking forward to showing her that I was worth it. I was "on track" (pun intended) to qualify for the state meet in the 200-meter dash, and I knew if I wanted a chance, I would have to get out of the blocks quickly and run harder than I had ever run. I had trained hard and I knew this was the year that I would be heading to the Girls' State Championship! With my future coach in the stands and my last chance to get to the state championship on the line, I got "ready" (with my spikes pressed firmly in the blocks) and "set" (I hoisted my hips so that my back was parallel to the track, with all of my weight being held by my fingertips). But before the starter could say "Go!" my nerves got the best of me. With the intent of "getting out the blocks" quickly, I took a step onto the track milliseconds before the gun went off. I false-started and was disqualified, with no recourse or second chance to get it right—all of my state track dreams were shattered in an instant. I was embarrassed, hurt, and thought my chances of success at the next level were shot like the blank that came out of the starter's gun. I felt horrible, but my future coach consoled me and affirmed that it was a mistake and wasn't the end of my athletic career. As hurt as I was, I felt comfort in her reassurance and looked forward to working with her.

A few weeks later, she was in my hometown for a camp and I was able to catch up with her. She showed me some of the workouts we would be doing and gave me an idea of what I should expect once we started training. I felt somewhat redeemed from the false-starting blunder and was even more excited about my journey as a collegiate track athlete. After spending time with her, I felt confident in her ability to help me develop and become a better runner. Despite the tragic end to my high school track career, I was very optimistic about the start of my collegiate athletic tenure.

About six weeks before the start of my freshman year, I attended a program on my college campus to help acclimate incoming freshmen to classes and earn a couple of credits in the process. Shortly into the program, I realized I needed to plan out my fall quarter class schedule in order for my academic journey to get off to a good start. My friend (who was also my teammate) and I walked over to talk to the academic advisor for track and field athletes. We went over our courses and in the middle of our consultation she greeted someone walking down the hallway and casually mentioned, "Oh, by the way, that's your new coach." She must have read the confusion and shock on my face because she called her back to introduce her to us. Our "new coach" popped her head in the door, said, "Hello, nice to meet you," and then left for lunch. I was floored and, in an instant, everything I envisioned about my future as a collegiate athlete changed. What happened? When? Who is this lady? Why did no one tell us that the person who recruited us would not be the person coaching us?

I had a major issue with being blindsided by a new coach and then not being properly introduced. It would have been nice to know who she was, what her vision was, and to learn more about her style of coaching before I was nonchalantly introduced to her in a fleeting moment. What was worse, was that she was just our event coach and there was a completely different person hired as the head coach. This change forced me to get comfortable with not just one, but *two* new coaches, neither of which took the time to even reach out to any of us incoming freshmen to let us know who they were. Neither the new event coach nor the new head coach reached out or sat down with any of us to let us know about anything that happened. I had the opportunity to at least meet my event coach (albeit by happenstance), but the head coach never once bothered to reach out to us *at all*.

The incoming freshman in our event group didn't know anything about either of the coaches, and it made me uneasy. This was not what I signed up for and I had a very difficult time adjusting to their leadership as a result. I had gotten comfortable with the previous coach, which is incredibly important in establishing trust, but with the new changes I didn't know what to expect. Looking back, I realize now that in my immaturity, this lack of trust manifested itself as stubbornness. I was perceived by my new coaches and my teammates as hard to coach, but deep down I was hurt and operating in a sense of uncertainty about my future as an athlete—and as a student. I didn't know it at the time, but I later realized that I couldn't shake the lack of trust caused primarily by the lack of communication by the coaching staff. Unfortunately, it led to two years of me being bitter on the inside and probably many years of being misunderstood and perceived negatively by my team and coaches on the outside. I regret that some of my actions may have caused issues in our team dynamic and I am remorseful in my belligerent attitude toward my event coach. However, it was a learning moment that taught me a lot about the importance of communication in leadership.

The summer before my junior year of college, I received a phone call at my parent's house. On the other end was a very enthusiastic-sounding voice introducing herself as my new event coach. She told me her background and outlined her expectations. When I got back on the track in the fall, I had to push through some of the hardest workouts I had ever done, and there were many uncomfortable demands I had to endure. But there was a sense of trust that had been established from the beginning of this new relationship that helped me look beyond what may have seemed crazy to achieve—some of my personal best times on the track. It seems like such a small detail, but it made a huge difference in my performances.

My experiences as a track athlete and the memory of this uncomfortable situation gave me a new perspective on leadership and helped me facilitate a change in teaching personnel when I became a teacher. I know how hard it is to adjust to a new leader and I placed a great deal of emphasis on helping the transition go as smoothly as possible when I had to change positions from seventh-grade math teacher to sixth through eighth-grade math support teacher in the middle of the school year, I knew the students deserved better than them just showing up on a Monday morning with a new teacher standing in front of them. My principal wanted to send out an email on Sunday letting the parents know the change had been made, but that didn't sit well with me, so I requested we approach the transition differently. I had been to a restorative practices training and was able to use the techniques learned to create a circle in which I shared the news with them. It was important for me that both the principal (who made the decision), as well as their new teacher, would be a part of the circle also. This helped to minimize the trauma of "losing" their teacher and helped them embrace the idea of learning from someone different. Many of them were upset and some even cried. It hurt me to see some of their reactions, but it was done in a way that they had the opportunity to express their feelings—good, bad, or otherwise. I cared too much about them for me not to respect their emotions and allow them to be blindsided by the change, even if it made it more difficult for me to leave.†

POWER POINT: ESTABLISH AND COMMUNICATE EXPECTATIONS AND POLICIES CLEARLY AND EFFECTIVELY—BEFORE A CRISIS HITS

For a short period of time, I served as the head administrator of a small charter school. While serving in this capacity, I was charged with the task of making very difficult decisions in the absence of the

---

†*Over time and off the track, I grew to respect and appreciate my first collegiate event coach, as she was a beautiful person inside and out. She was young, fresh out of college, and didn't deserve the hard time I gave her, because it really wasn't her fault. Ultimately, it should have been the head coach's job to communicate personnel changes and introduce the new event coach to the team. Unfortunately, I didn't know any better and made a lot of mistakes in the process. She tragically passed away in 2009, but it is my hope and prayer that she knew she made a positive impact on my life and despite our differences and difficulties, I learned a lot and became a better person as a result. May God bless her soul and may her legacy of kindness, care for others, and greatness live on forever.*

school's founder and director. I thought the director understood I made decisions based on what was always in the best interest of the students. However, the contradictory and confusing guidance I received made me question my leadership at the time. I have since learned that just because others may have unrealistic expectations, doesn't mean I was inadequate in my ability to serve in leadership, but at the time, it really caused me to wrack my brain and wonder.

I once had a situation in which a five-year-old kindergartner fell on the playground and split her forehead open. The little girl was scared, bleeding, and in pain, and I didn't have time to consult with the director—a decision needed to be made quickly. When the student was brought inside, I made an ice pack, wiped the blood, and called her mother. I wanted to know if she wanted me to call the ambulance or wait for her to come pick her up. As a leader, I knew I had to consider two groups of people—the kindergartners who saw her fall and might have been even more fearful with the sight and knowledge of an ambulance, and her parents who may not have liked the idea of her riding the ambulance without them and who could have been charged a fee for the ride. I didn't think about reaching out to my director at the moment, because I had an emergency on my hands and needed to make a decision quickly. I thought that if the mother agreed to the ambulance, then it would be okay and I could handle the aftermath of the terrified kids later, but if not, she would have had the option to pick her up and do what she thought was best for her child. I was thankful the mother told me she was on her way and would take her to the emergency room. As we waited, I talked to the little girl to make sure she was coherent and was not having a concussion or some other type of brain injury that would cause memory loss or challenges with her cognition. I also wanted to ensure that she didn't go into shock, which could be ultimately worse than the injury itself. (Someone had done this for me when I was in a near-fatal car accident and I'm convinced it helped save my life, and at the very least, my sanity.) My heart was pounding out of my chest, but this sweet young baby was so brave and when her mom arrived, I knew she would be okay.

After she left, I called the school's director to let her know what happened and to find out if there was any administrative paperwork I needed to file and, to my dismay, she *snapped*! She was incredibly angry and questioned why I didn't call the ambulance. She went on and on and told me that if there was ever a situation like that again, I should call the ambulance and then call the parent afterward. I thought it was a stupid solution, but I said, "Okay," and moved on. I didn't want to argue with her. This was *her* school (as she made a point to emphasize whenever she could), and if that's how she wanted to roll, then whatever. But I also knew that in my position, I would likely have to make more on-the-fly decisions and needed to figure out how to best handle the situation if something like that happened again.

Later in the same school year, there was an incident in which I was teaching a class (we had limited staff, so even though I was the head administrator, I still had to teach two classes), and two of the older students had gotten into a disagreement with a teacher in another class. I called them down to my classroom to see if I could de-escalate the situation, but they were adamant about walking out and they left the school on their own. I reached out to their parents and the director, whom I could not reach, so once again I had to make a decision based on the circumstances that were in front of me. I had a class full of young adults who I could not leave unsupervised and there was no one to either cover my class or chase after them. These students were now walking the streets during the school day without supervision themselves, so, I called the police. I needed to get somebody to locate them and bring them back to the school safely because I did not have the capacity to do so. The director called as I was in the middle of teaching and told me, "*Nobody* calls the police on *my* school." I told her I really didn't have much of a choice but again she went on and on about how this made her look bad and that her students aren't criminals, yadda-yadda-yah. Okay, whatever. *Do* call the ambulance, but *don't* call the police? I was confused and annoyed by the contradictions in her directives and was worn out from trying to figure out how to make the best judgments in situations like these. If a clear plan of action had been established and shared with me from the very beginning, I would have known the expectations and operated accordingly. If you are leading team members who have to make critical decisions in a split second, please implement consistent protocols that result in intelligent solutions.

PAIN POINT: PASSING THE BUCK OF LEADERSHIP TO OTHERS AND NOT ACCEPTING RESPONSIBILITY FOR YOUR OWN DECISIONS

When school principals choose to use their assistant or vice principals to serve as gatekeepers of communication (especially when dealing with grievances or complaints), it hinders their ability to build relationships and makes them seem unapproachable. It is important for leaders to recognize which issues should be delegated to their assistants and which ones will ultimately end up back on their desks to deal with anyway. If the situation is one in which the leader will have to make the final decision, they should speak with the subordinate directly about their decision, why it makes sense for the organization, and what alternate solutions they may have for the person with the grievance. By refusing to speak directly with people either to stall them out, buy time, or wear them down, weakens the leader's authority and could create a hostile situation that doesn't have to be. It is not an ideal way to establish or maintain favorable rapport.

In an all-school preplanning faculty session, I had a former principal say, "If you have any issues with me, you need to bring them to me directly, because anything you say to my administrative staff will come back to me anyway." This was a petty and cryptic statement, more akin to what I would expect to come out of the mouth of a high school student looking to pick a fight rather than an accomplished educator with a doctorate degree trying to establish a line of communication with her teaching staff. What's worse was that these words were completely contradictory to the way she operated. Instead of meeting directly with teachers, she would push people off to her administrators because she "trusted their judgment" and "let them handle her issues." By contrast, she had an expectation that people should come directly to her with their grievances. How? How did she expect this to happen? She was not direct with others, so she could not expect them to be direct with her. Relationships require reciprocity, and there was no way she would ever get her staff to open up if she wasn't willing to have direct conversations with them.

PAIN POINT: BEING INTIMIDATED BY YOUR SUBORDINATE'S BACKGROUND OR EXPERTISE INSTEAD OF USING IT TO BUILD A STRONG TEAM

I have seen far too many situations in which a school, team, organization, or department had the potential to grow and improve exponentially, but ultimately fell apart because leadership felt threatened by the knowledge base and/or experiences of their subordinates. Unfortunately, this is rooted in jealousy and an irrational fear that these individuals might someday take their jobs. In these situations, the leader often harasses, makes unreasonable demands, and creates an uncomfortable working environment for the person on their team they are intimidated by, which drives that person to exit. I know sometimes this can be difficult for an administrator to admit to themselves, but if you are a leader in a school (or any other organization for that matter), please take some time to reflect introspectively and ask if there is anyone on your team you feel intimidated by. Then, ask yourself if you have spent adequate time getting to know this person. What are their motivations, goals, and strengths? How can they benefit your team and actually be positioned to make you look good? The greatest leaders allow their employees to shine in the areas in which they excel in order to build the team optimally. Their contribution to the school, team, or department will translate into a win for the leader who ultimately gives them space to be empowered in their strengths. It is a win-win for everyone involved.

POWER POINT: OPERATING WITH GRACE FOR OTHERS, ESPECIALLY IN A PANDEMIC (OR OTHER UNUSUAL CIRCUMSTANCES)

In a staff meeting during the pandemic's virtual learning period, I heard a kindergarten teacher say, "I'm having problems with the parents giving the kids snacks on camera." The administrator's response was to encourage them not to eat while on camera and to only eat or drink during designated breaks. I was outdone by the statement by the kindergarten teacher and even more taken aback by the administrator's response. Why was this even an issue? Who cares if the babies wanted to get something to eat while in class—they were at home for God's sake. Besides, granting small courtesies to students, like allowing them to eat or to be comfortable in their surroundings while attending class, can go a long way in building trust, rapport, and creating a desire to perform in excellence. On many occasions, students (especially those who are not intrinsically motivated to do well in school) will go out of their way to complete assignments and perform well for teachers that they like or want to impress. During this very critical time of the pandemic, providing freedoms to students (that they were likely going to take anyway, even if they weren't given) may have helped keep them motivated to engage in the distance learning environment. It worked well in the classes I taught.

A lot of my students were boys with younger sisters. They showed up to class engaged and ready to work and sometimes their baby sisters would come into the frame wanting attention from their brothers. I noticed that the young men would encourage them to leave the space or send them away, but I would stop them. I told them, "That's your sister and if nothing else, they need to know you are their protector. They are more than welcome to join you in class—they may learn something in the process." I wanted to be clear with my students that I honored their spaces and their homes and if that meant I had toddlers joining our class sessions, it was perfectly fine with me. It was during these times, the students became even more engaged, and it helped me to build relationships with them.

Adults are no different. When we work for a company or supervisor that goes out of their way to show how much we are valued, we tend to work harder and do all we can to meet or exceed expectations.

PAIN POINT: HAVING EXPECTATIONS FOR STUDENTS THAT YOU DON'T HAVE FOR TEACHERS

In the same meeting in which the teacher was expressing her grievances about her students eating on screen, there were teachers eating their lunches and drinking water and coffee on screen. How in the world can administrators have an expectation from students they don't even have from their teachers? If a teacher can eat and/or drink on screen, then I don't see anything wrong with allowing their students to do the same. This is just one example, but we cannot operate by the "do as I say, not as I do" philosophy in this day and age. If teachers have an expectation of students, then those teachers cannot hypocritically do the opposite.

POWER POINT: RESPECTING AND HAVING CONCERN FOR YOUR EMPLOYEES' FAMILY MEMBERS AND CIRCUMSTANCES

Work-life balance is critical for optimal performance, especially for parents and those who are caregivers to people they love. When employees' families are thriving, they can work with a clear heart and mind that translates into optimal performance. By contrast, when teachers and staff spend their time with a mind occupied with worry about their family members, it causes undue stress and poor performance.

One of the best examples of an administrator meeting the needs of his teachers that I have witnessed was when there was a wave of Covid-19 that hit especially hard and many daycare centers closed down. I knew of a principal who actually allowed his teachers to bring their young children (two to three years of age) to work with them. It was so cute to see the little ones in line with their parents' students and it all worked out well. This demonstrated to all of the teachers that they were not only valued, but that the administration was sensitive to their needs and accommodated them accordingly. Schools are places for children and small children should be made welcome in those environments as long as they are being properly cared for by their parents while there.

Last but certainly not least . . .

POWER POINT: LEADING WITH HIGH EXPECTATIONS WRAPPED IN CARE

This power point requires a very special gift that many people do not innately have, but could learn and cultivate with proper training and practice. Those who follow this piece of advice can master every other power point on the list and eliminate pain points in their leadership practices. This power point is rooted in service and care for others, thinking of what it's like to be in another person's shoes, and treating others in a way that they are honored and respected.

Far too often, the atmosphere of a classroom is negatively impacted by the mood and attitude of a teacher. For example, if a teacher has a bad morning, ends up being late, and then gets a cold reprimand by their administrator upon arriving at work, this could result in the teacher being angry and/or frustrated and taking this out on their students. Instead of an attack on their tardiness or threatening to write the teacher up, a good way to approach this concern is to say,

"I noticed you have been struggling with getting here on time. Is everything okay? How can I help?" This wording presents a way to break down barriers of difficulty without embarrassing the person being addressed. It acknowledges the behavior/issue in question while at the same time showing them that they are cared about and that you are willing to work with them to help resolve the issue. This method of leadership is rare, but has the power to transform schools for the better. Kindness is contagious and when it's enveloped in effective leadership, its trickle-down effect is transformative in the best possible way.

Administrators can be authoritative without being rude, harsh, dismissive, or condescending. Everyone in education is going through a hard enough time and it is a great time to practice grace and kindness. The fragrant sweetness of nectar is a magnet to honeybees, which in turn produce delicious and nutritious honey for all to enjoy, but flies are drawn to feces and are a nuisance for all in their presence. Is your leadership style one that attracts producers of excellence or does it give off a stench that creates swarms of pestilence? It is my hope that as leaders, you choose to establish your school as a beautiful flower bed rather than a rotten dung heap of chaos.

CHAPTER 6
TEACHERS R . . .

Called. What does that mean? Dictionary.com defines a call as "to summon by or as if by divine command," which is an accurate meaning. But for teachers, I am going to take it a step further and describe it as a role in which they **C**ultivate **A**spirations in **L**earners for a **L**ifetime (CALL). The call to teach is deep and unique and powerful and humbling. If you are not a teacher, please know that regardless of how you may perceive them, most of them do not enter this field because the money is good or to get on other people's nerves. They felt a tug in their hearts to make an impact, to show their care for young people, and to share their passions and expertise with others. They have an intention to do good things. They answered a call and picked up the PHONE—**P**ossibilities to **H**arness **O**pportunities and **N**egate mediocrity through **E**ducation—to serve children of all ages and even adults.

Some teachers' approach and style may not work for all children (all things are not for all people) and there are some pretty bad apples out there who really should not be in classrooms at all. (Please know I am not advocating for horrible teachers, and those who have not been called should find another profession.) But for the most part, teachers give the best of themselves every day to make the lives of other people better. One of the most intelligent and eloquent speakers I know said that one of the hardest teachers he ever had made him memorize a poem each week. He talked about how much he hated it at the time, but that it helped him build strong skills he still uses to this day. Some of the teachers who are the hardest and seem like the worst during the time we are in their classes are actually some of the best because they require high standards of excellence they refuse to back down from.

If you are reading this and you are *not* a teacher, but you're a parent, I want you to know that the countless hours and time teachers put in for *your* child and for the children of others is immeasurable. One of the best things you can do to enhance your child's educational experience is to partner *with* teachers and not work against them. They are not perfect, and they need your support. If you are an administrator, I want you to know that teachers are your most valuable asset, and your encouragement and appreciation goes a long way in giving them the fuel they need to keep going when times get rough. If you are a student, I pray you have (or have had) at least one teacher you feel truly cared about you. If you did, this is your reminder to give them a call, send them a card, or flowers. If you are a current student, act like you have some sense in class and give them your best, because that's what they give to you every day, even on their worst days.

As the daughter of a retired teacher and coach, I was a witness to the amount of time and energy my father poured into students and athletes over a forty-year period. As the sister of a teacher who has been teaching and coaching for over twenty years, I have had the honor of seeing the impact of my brother's work on his current and former students and athletes. As the sister-in-law of an elementary school teacher, I learn about how much her students love her and enjoy being in her class. As the mother of four very different children, I appreciate the time teachers spend to help my children learn and grow every day. As a student, I was a high achiever and worked my butt off in the classroom, but I sometimes gave my teachers a hard time despite the care they gave to me. As an administrator, I worked hard to make sure that teachers were supported in the best way I could. As a former teacher, I see teachers. I see their long hours and their sacrifices. I hurt when they hurt, and my heart is filled with joy when they experience triumphs in their classrooms and with student success.

If you are a teacher and have answered the CALL, regardless of whether it is an emergency call or the call of a lifetime, I want to thank you. Thank you for the tireless hours you spend preparing lessons. Thank you for the love you pour into your students. Thank you for spending your own money and resources to provide when your skool is unable (or unwilling) to. Thank you for all that you do—this is my love letter to you.

DEAR INCREDIBLE SELFLESS HUMAN (A.K.A. TEACHER)

When I answered the PHONE of my calling to teach, smartphones didn't exist. There was no caller ID or app to help guide or enhance my calling experience. I wasn't able to look at a screen that would tell me if the call was a "Scam Likely" and I could choose to ignore it. I really didn't know what I was getting myself into, but I feel honored to have been called and I'm glad I answered that call—and I'm glad you did too. This is the story of my call to teach. Maybe some of it resonates with you and some of it may be very different than the path you are on. Either way, I hope you know whether you are on a Lifetime Call (in which you spend your entire career dedicated to educating young minds) or on an Emergency Call (in which you step in when you are needed most), the time you spend in the classroom is one of the most important decisions you can make. I hope you are encouraged and empowered to continue to be your greatest self, not just for your students but because this work is what you are called to do.

This calling has compelled you to pour your gifts and talents into young people that will have a ripple effect reaching generations into eternity. I want you to know that your work is not in vain and not meaningless. I want you to know what you say, how you show up, and the life you speak into your students everyday matters. At this point in history, teaching may be the most difficult and important profession that exists. Kids come to schools with all sorts of baggage, carrying some of the greatest traumas and burdens, and unfortunately, teachers often get the brunt of those hurts. At the same time, teachers get the privilege of helping to be the salve for those pains and give them hope for their futures. Students may not ever come back and say hello or even thank you for all that you gave them, but believe me, whatever you have poured into them has the power to impact them in ways you could have never imagined.

To be honest, I never knew I was capable of teaching prior to starting my journey as an educator. I often turned my nose up and even rolled my eyes when I was out in public and I was in the presence of a child acting a fool or screaming his or her head off. I never thought I had the patience or the desire to even work with children. I had done a couple of volunteer gigs in which I worked with kids, and it was cool, but I definitely didn't think I had the ability to be stuck in a classroom with them all day. I was an exceptional student, but I also know I gave my teachers fits sometimes in the classroom and I did not want to be bothered with some version of myself (or some of my other classmates) as my student. However, I did have a significant interest in becoming an academic advisor/counselor. As a student-athlete at a school that took most people five years to graduate, I found a way to do it in four years instead and even showed others how to do the same.

During my senior year of college, I saw an opportunity to get a teacher certification prior to graduating that I wanted to take advantage of. It was a partnership between two state schools that would have allowed me to become a certified math or science teacher. I thought it would be great for me, especially since I had so many elective credit hours I needed to fill in. I never had the intention of teaching, but I figured, *Hey, why not?* There were no other interesting classes to fill up those hours. At worst, if I didn't have the job I wanted when I graduated, I would at least have a certificate that would open the opportunity for a decent job. Upon inquiring, however, I learned that in order to be eligible, I had to be a math, science, or engineering major. As a business major, I didn't qualify, so I just decided in my mind and heart that maybe teaching wasn't meant for me and took a bunch of random hodge-podge electives so I could meet the requirements to graduate and get on with my life. But for two years after I graduated college, I wandered aimlessly, unable to find my career footing, and I felt purposeless. I had some decent jobs but, in my mind, they never matched the college degree I worked so hard for, and I struggled to feel like I was doing meaningful work.

Right around this time, a national teacher shortage was taking place. In my home state, a program was created to help recruit new teachers to the profession and fill in the gaps. I had been spinning my wheels trying to figure out what to do with my life since I had graduated, and this presented an open door for a purposeful career. I really thought I would be best suited as a guidance counselor, since it was the closest job to being an academic advisor I could think of. But I wasn't having any luck finding or being hired for either of those jobs so I thought perhaps I should give teaching another try. It was in my blood, and I really had not thought about or recognized it prior to that. I was born into a family of educators, but I never had a genuine interest in teaching until the Teach for Georgia opportunity was presented. At that point, I had been out of school for two years, had bounced from job to job, and even attempted grad school. I wanted to truly make a difference in the lives of others. So, despite my initial pushback to pursue education as a career, I applied for the program to see if it could be a good fit and my answer to the call to teach began.

Out of over six hundred applicants to the program, I was one of only a select few chosen to participate. The program's director was ecstatic and told me that I had the "look" of a teacher. This was my first bit of confirmation I was headed down the right path. The program was designed for aspiring teachers to take minicourses for six weeks to prepare them for the classroom and the participants would then enroll in school to complete their certification requirements. About halfway through the initial part of the program, I figured this would be a good move for me and that I needed to decide what level of teaching would be best. I knew I definitely didn't want to teach elementary school because bodily fluids are not my thing. Elementary-aged kids are super cute, but the snot, boogers, occasional urine, and vomit that come along with them are not. Gross! So, high school it was going to be. I was ready and looking forward to becoming a cool, young high school teacher who would also serve as a cheerleading and/or track coach. I thought to myself, *Yeah, that's a plan I could manage*. I interviewed at a high school that reminded me of my own alma mater and fell in love with it. I would be teaching English and I could already envision working there: cheer coach, track coach, yearbook advisor—yes, yes, yes—count me in!

There was only one problem: I didn't have enough college credits in English to teach high school English, so I had to compromise and get "stuck in the middle" for middle school language arts. Crazy thing is . . . I should have gravitated toward middle school in the first place. It was a naturally great fit for me. My favorite school years are from the two years I was in junior high—my seventh and eighth-grade years. It was during those years I truly thrived at school! My favorite teacher was my seventh-grade language arts teacher, Mrs. Linda Miller, who taught us all to become "hookers" (how to "hook" our readers with writing that draw them in), and we had so many opportunities to enhance the academic learning we were getting in the classroom. In seventh grade, I won the city-wide spelling bee, made the cheerleading squad, and was inducted into the National Junior Honor Society. By the time I got to the eighth grade, I was not only involved in almost every extracurricular activity you could think of, I was in leadership positions for most of them as well. Those were some great years and I learned so much and enjoyed my time. I cherished those moments deep in the recesses of my memories and felt I could remember them well enough to be relatable to the students I would be teaching. Being "stuck in the middle" as a middle school teacher was the perfect fit.

I was hired to teach seventh-grade language arts in the summer of 2002 and was becoming more and more excited as the first day of school got closer. I purchased books I thought my students would enjoy reading to serve as a part of my classroom library and hung posters of pop culture icons to keep them inspired. I never thought to ask for financial help to get my classroom in order because I thought it was a part of the job and I was happy to do it. I knew the return on my investment would be the opportunity to change minds and lives for the better and that every child was worth it. Right before the kids were set to embark on their new school year, I went to the school parking lot at night to reflect . . . and pray. I didn't take this new venture lightly. It was not the same as tying shoelaces for customers at an athletic footwear and apparel retail establishment or working for my old college's cable network. These parents were sending their kids to *me* (and their other teachers) so they could learn something that would help mold them into the people they would become in the future. My every step and lesson had to be calculated—I didn't want to mess this up! I knew how valuable those children were, even though I had not met them yet, and that it was my job to ensure they were better at the end of the year than when they started.

As a first-year teacher, I had my moments in which I made mistakes, but all in all, I thought I did pretty well. I used music lyrics to enhance our poetry lessons, brought in guest speakers, and even participated in the faculty-student flag football game (which was another way for me to let the kids know that although I was young, I was to be respected without question). I developed a good relationship with most of my students (hey, you can't please everyone) and hoped I was a positive role model and influence in their lives. By the end of my first year, I had enrolled in the teacher certification program and was making good progress toward getting certified *and* obtaining a master's degree in education. With an offer to come back for a second year of teaching, I thought I had finally found my groove. It was at this point I realized that I really did have a heart for children and I wanted to do my very best for them. I love and nurture all children as if they are my own and even before I had given birth to my very own babies, I mothered my students and the kids I came in contact with on a daily basis. Some of my students saw me as a second mom, auntie, or even big sister, and I fully embraced my role as someone they looked up to. The heartwork is what I loved most about being a teacher and I honestly thought I had answered a Lifetime Call and that I would retire from this profession.

Certainly, as a teacher, I had my flaws. My classroom could get pretty loud, and as a "free-spirited non-planner," I had difficulty with the rigid, boring structure of the curriculum I was given to work with. On many days, especially as a language arts teacher, I really just wanted to play music, read excerpts, or show video clips, and have meaningful discussions about whatever we heard, watched, or listened to. I loved projects and wished there were more creative ways to bring the curriculum to life using these methods, but because of my required teaching objectives and set curriculum structure, I was beyond stuck in the middle—I was just plain "stuck." Stuck with huge stacks of papers to grade; stuck with the boring lesson plans and textbook of our prescribed curriculum; and stuck feeling like I wasn't making as much of an impact as I hoped to. It was this part of teaching that was burdensome and a source of stress. Although I liked teaching, these requirements of my job were an indication that maybe I wasn't "called" like the many teachers I knew who had been in it for the long haul.

As a part of our statewide test prep, teachers would work daily with our homeroom students on a variety of different subjects to help them get ready. I recall the times when math was the focus and found myself doing a pretty good job of helping kids understand the concepts. I loved language arts as a student and the idea of the creative nature of the subject as a teacher, but I thought perhaps I could be a "better" teacher if I taught mathematics instead. Math is pretty straightforward, and although there is room for creativity, once a kid's confidence is built and they learn how to solve problems effectively, they can be on the road to mastery. One of the middle school certification requirements was to select two disciplines as a teaching focus. I was already teaching language arts, but these homeroom mini-lessons helped me learn that math would be my other focal point as a classroom teacher.

I was great at solving issues that involved teaching and learning in the classroom. Recognizing how to manipulate the content to meet the needs of the unique learners in my class was something I did pretty well. Skool and skool-system-imposed restrictions were incredibly frustrating, but I always found a way around them. For me, I had to find ways to help my students get what they needed by any means necessary, and I went out of my way to do so. It led to a conflict with my assistant principal/curriculum director about teaching grammar, but in the end, the students benefited from my nonconformance with the curriculum.

Schools and systems like order, so my inability to provide routines and some sort of consistent structure, while allowing children to exist willy-nilly in the classroom was highly frowned upon in the teaching profession. Deep down, I felt that schools and school systems were too restrictive, and I had a difficult time finding the balance between allowing children the freedom to be themselves and maintaining a sense of order that would be most conducive to their learning.

However, there was a political and systematic storm brewing I was unaware of, threatening my call to teach with bureaucracy that was hiding behind the guise of accountability and the elevation of standards of excellence. It was a much larger threat to my continuity in teaching than my frustrations and fixable flaws. When the No Child Left Behind Act of 2001 made its way to our school, teachers who lacked certification were on the chopping block, so my contract was not renewed. It was then that I learned that for me, teaching was not a Lifetime Call, but instead an Emergency Call—one for a specific purpose, at an appointed time. The call was disconnected, but not forever. This was a call I would answer several more times throughout my career in education before I finally recognized that as a teacher, my number was like 911 and I was the emergency services team that would come to the rescue of schools in need.

Those Emergency Calls included teaching a life skills course in a charter school, math teacher at my old junior high (which had since become a middle school), seventh-grade math teacher, and sixth, seventh, and eighth-grade math support teacher. In my last call to teach, I "clicked over" from the call in which I was teaching middle school students in a math-support class to another call, teaching talented and gifted elementary students. Although I had never taught elementary school students, the position was part teacher and part administrator, and it ultimately led to the best fit I had as a teacher. In addition to being called to the profession, teachers should also be placed in environments and situations that best fit their strengths and abilities. I give credit and thanks to my administrators for recognizing my strengths and placing me in a role better fit for my skill set.

I ultimately "hung up" the call to teach and answered a different call in the field of education. I probably would have stayed, but I lacked peace and an infinitely better opportunity opened the door for my true calling, in which I can operate with my full range of gifts without stress or restrictions. It took me a very long time to get to this place in my career, but I would not be able to thrive in my current role if I had not answered the call to teach. It gave me the experience and foundation to fully understand the enormity of the classroom teacher role. My time as a teacher taught me so much about myself and helped me understand the mighty work that teachers do every day. Most importantly, I had the opportunity to touch young people's lives in an incredible way.

If you are a teacher, you are called to do great things for your students. You are called to serve. You are called to fill in as a parent, nurse, counselor, confidant, and—in some cases—hairdresser, referee, wardrobe stylist, and life coach. There is so much weighing on a teacher's call that sometimes it can be overwhelming. I know so many who have left the profession and many others who threaten to do so, but (if possible) don't hang up and don't give up! The work you do is so meaningful, and many lives are depending on your presence, your love, and your wisdom in the classroom.

So how do you remain on the call without getting weary and wanting to hang up the PHONE? There are many professional development options that can help guide you through your calling and empower you through your day-to-day life as a teacher, but this is not one of them. You can Google ways to build better lesson plans or implement Social-Emotional Learning (SEL), but the empowerment guide I present to you over the next few pages is a collection of some of my firsthand experiences I hope will inspire you as you continue on your call. I share stories from a teacher's perspective, parent's perspective, and student's perspective that serve as proof that teaching matters.

This is my "SmartPHONE" Guide for empowerment on the call. Because from teacher to teacher, we both know the real way to outsmart the system is to out-heart the system. There are lessons and curriculum written on your heart only you can give. There is (or has been) a child in your classroom who will be the first in his or her family to graduate from college because of you. There is a child in your classroom who will save lives because you said something that inspired her. There is a child in your classroom who will break a generational curse and become an exceptional father to his children because he watched your example. These are the intangibles that systems cannot mandate or regulate. These are the outcomes that data cannot measure. This is what makes you powerful. This is what keeps you empowered.

ALIDA DAVIS ABDULLAH

A DAUGHTER'S DOTING ON HER DEDICATED DAD

My exposure and understanding of excellence in teaching started long before I ever stepped foot in a classroom, either as a student or teacher. My father, Wallace Davis, answered the call while training for the NFL. He had already beaten the odds and played for the Minnesota Vikings and Atlanta Falcons, and he was working to get picked up by the New Orleans Saints—a lofty dream for a young Black man who grew up in the Jim Crow South. The principal of a local high school had been watching him and appreciated his work ethic and drive. He knew my dad would be perfect—his skills and drive, coupled with his vitality and influential nature, made him the perfect candidate to teach and coach. He asked my dad to join his staff, but it wasn't an easy sell. My father loved playing football and a taste of NFL success had been on the tip of his tongue. He truly desired to make a name for himself as a professional football player and had a difficult time letting it go. Eventually, the school principal won him over, and my dad traded in his cleats and helmet for a whistle and some too-tight coaching shorts. (It was the '70s, what can I say?) Once he stepped foot into his role as a PE Teacher, head track coach, and assistant football coach, he exchanged his own dreams and aspirations in order to help others fulfill theirs. The year I was born, he was promoted from an assistant to head football coach, head track coach, and athletic director at the high school I would eventually graduate from, and his legendary teaching and coaching career began.

My father is one of the greatest teachers I've ever known. Not just because he's my dad, but because the impact he made on the lives of his students and players is proof. He spent his days as a teacher and coach committed to ensuring he brought the best out of all the kids he worked with. He would leave the house at seven a.m. and wouldn't return until ten or eleven o'clock some nights. This was not just his job—he truly cultivated aspirations in young people through his calling. Throughout his career, he was able to teach, coach, and mentor students who graduated to become Super Bowl champions, doctors, lawyers, teachers, coaches, business owners, community leaders, and changemakers. Along with my mother, his wife of fifty-three years at the time of this publication, he set an exceptional example of what a loving husband and strong marriage looked like. Her devotion to assist in his calling was unmatched—she made dinner for his athletes, hosted other coaches and families in our home, and even fed our track team (and some members of other track teams too) during those long, all-day competitions. Together, they gave young people in our community "relationship goals" and established a high standard of excellence upon which many successful marriages were modeled. He often laments that he didn't spend as much time with my brother and I because he spent so much time with other people's children. However, it is this trait that I have always admired about him and has served as a template for me and my brother's success.

Many of his athletes had odds stacked against them, but my father has an incredible ability to develop a kid's potential and make others believe in them also. So many college and professional doors were opened for his student-athletes because he convinced others to give them a chance. My father's dedication to teaching and coaching helped make my brother an exceptional teacher and coach who has also been instrumental in helping countless student-athletes achieve their goals. My father led by example, and through his vocation I saw the power of being there for others and the powerful impact of answering a Lifetime Call to teach.

A STUDENT'S SNAPSHOT AND TEACHER TRIBUTE

When I was a student, I really did love school, but I was also pretty energetic. In kindergarten and first grade, I was fairly mellow, but by the time I got to the second grade, I was a giggly, vivacious, "chatterboxing" ball of joy. The high achiever in me ensured I got all of my work done in excellence, but the busybody in me made sure I had plenty of "extra credit" to go along with it. I wrote lots of sentences to the tune of "I will not talk in class," held dictionaries for long periods of time (but never seemed to get beautiful Michelle Obama arms to go along with it), and even had to sit under my teacher's desk. By today's standards, these consequences might be considered harsh or even abusive, but in my mind, it was better than getting popped with a ruler. I know I used to "cut up" and I appreciate all my teachers endured while I was in their classes. Every one of my teachers, good, bad, or otherwise, poured into me in a way that has shaped me into the person I have become, and for that, I am truly grateful.

They don't know how important they were to me and, though I haven't really kept in touch,

I hope the following tribute helps my teachers know that I appreciate them so much:

In kindergarten, Mrs. Rutledge let me stay awake during naptime so I could read and write.

Mrs. Wynne expanded my reading skills and helped my academic journey take flight.

Ms. Dillard was my favorite in the second grade, and in her class, I would always put on a show.

I was her "Sugar-Booger" and was so happy to have her two years in a row.

Mrs. Mims called me a Wiggly-Worm and I gave Mrs. Strozier so much drama.

Mrs. Walker took me in and loved on me when I lost my grandmama.

Ms. Martin was tough, and in her class, I earned my first B.

My parents were upset, but it made me resilient and I learned responsibility.

And I can't forget about Mrs. Guinne and Mrs. Boutte who also prepared me for my junior high days.

Mrs. Linda Miller gave me the tools to develop a good "hook."

Yep, I became a "hooker"—it enticed you to pick up this book.

All my junior high teachers provided me with experiences I'll never forget.

Those years owe me nothing—I truly have no regrets.

Through our triumphs and adversities, my high school teachers taught us so much "On Da Hill."

Our teachers were our greatest resource—they were extraordinary, not run of the mill.

I will forever be grateful for all my teachers, and what they did for me year after year.

For all the lessons they taught me from my childhood into my own education career.

No matter what talents and gifts we use or whatever our occupation.

Let's not forget to honor our teachers and show our appreciation.

For being the wind beneath our wings, giving us the lift to fly high and soar.

And answering the call inspiring us to become all that we can . . . and so much more.

STUDENTS INSPIRE TEACHERS TOO

As a teacher, I had the incredible honor of working with so many young people that served as confirmation I was the right person in the right place at the right time on the call. When No Child Left Behind left me behind without a job, I lost contact with many of those students. For a long time, I wondered what happened to these wonderful kids whose potential for greatness inspired me.

One of those kids used to call me "mom." In my early years of teaching, I was young and felt more like one of the students than I did a teacher. Adulting was new to me, and I can't say I was fully ready to embrace it. But as the head of a classroom, even though I still felt like a teenager, I had to operate as an adult—you know, "fake it 'til I make it." Well, it must have worked, because I had one student who one day said, "Hey, Ms. Davis—can I call you 'mom'?"

I was barely old enough to be these kids' sibling, much less a mom, but I said, "Sure, that's fine. Why do you want to call me 'mom' anyway?"

His matter-of-fact response was, "You are like a mom to me." My heart was touched, and I was actually honored that he saw me in this way. He was one of my students who was always vibrant, came to class, and gave it his best every day, and was an incredibly talented writer.

Another one of my students was always a phenomenon to me because it is really difficult to be the "cool kid" in middle school. As a seventh grader, I was battling awkwardness, pimple-facedness, too-large teeth, and terrible hair, so I was in awe of her ability to navigate the world around her with such finesse and maturity. She was the one that all the girls wanted to be like and all the boys had a crush on. It was hard for me to believe that she was only thirteen. As a student, she worked hard in class and always contributed insightful perspectives in classroom discussions. She was a leader amongst her peers and didn't seem to succumb to the pitfalls of peer pressure—she kept a level head and encouraged those around her to do the same.

Then I had a student who always operated in excellence, no matter the assignment or format in which it was given. She was the most well-behaved child in any of my classes and on those rough days when my students were running amok and I wanted to give up on them *and* me, I always drew strength and believed there was hope for the future because of her calm and gentle spirit. She was quiet, but kind to others and one of the sweetest and wise-hearted students I'd ever taught. During that time, she told me I was one of her favorite teachers and I could hardly believe it. I honestly didn't think I was as good of a teacher as she deserved to have and wished I could have been even better.

For many years after leaving that group of students, I wondered what happened to them. After adulting truly took hold of me and I became a wife and mother, I became so focused on my own family that I really didn't think my former students even remembered me. Until one day in the mall, I saw the "cool kid" and she came up to me and gave me a huge hug. She told me she had been looking for me for years and I was shocked by this revelation. Although she spent some time in college, she was answering her call to become a police officer and would be graduating from the police academy soon and wanted me to be there. I was honored to be invited, and with pride, I piled my pregnant belly, two small children, and brother-in-law (who was visiting from out of town) in the car and drove more than one hundred miles to her ceremony. I got the chance to see her receive her credentials and ushered into her career as a cop and I couldn't have been prouder! She served in that role for over ten years and is now pursuing her law degree.

I somehow stumbled upon my "gentle-spirit" student on social media. I learned that she is an early childhood educator who loves what she does. I follow her posts and get a chance to see how amazing she is as a classroom teacher. When she graduated with her master's degree, I congratulated her and her response was, "You know, you are a teacher I will never forget . . . you are one of the reasons why I do what I do, teach! You made it fun to learn and I can only hope I have the same impact on my students!" It is so evident she is making an incredible impact on her students, and I feel confident that each one of her students will grow up to be amazing because she is a part of their lives. As a teacher, it doesn't get much better than this.

Then, one day, out of the blue, I got a LinkedIn message. It started off, "I don't know if you remember me . . ." but no introduction was necessary because I instantly knew who it was when I read his name. Tears of joy welled in my eyes as I read his message, and he explained how he found me based on what he remembered while he was in my class. My "first son" was doing well. He served honorably as a marine and was retiring as an officer. I shared my contact information with him, and we have been in touch ever since. He has been such a blessing to me. There are stories from back when he was in middle school that he remembers vividly and we talk often. He is now pursuing a master's degree in information technology.

These are just a few stories, but every single one of my former students is an inspiration to me and confirms that I answered the right call at the right time for the right people. I am honored to have had a small part in their success and my heart is filled with joy knowing those short Emergency Calls I answered have led to blessing others not just in their lives, but in the lives of everyone *they* touch. It is my hope that you, too, have students in your class that inspire you to show up to be your best self every day knowing your presence will set off a ripple in their lives that will be felt for many years. Although a human person may have made the call to tell you that you got the job, it was truly a divine calling that brought you to your position as a teacher. There is a greater force that compels you to do this work and orchestrates and aligns your environment, your circumstances, and the people in your life because *you* are who your students need for such a time as this.

A PARENT'S HEART OF GRATITUDE

After witnessing teacher excellence as a daughter, being the beneficiary of teaching excellence as a student, and serving my version of teaching excellence in the profession, I became a parent, and like his mother before him, my son was quite a handful in the classroom. In many environments, he is what I would call "educationally oppressed" because many skoolz and systems did not know how to handle his overly active brilliance and didn't know what to do with all of his pent-up energy when he was being told to sit still and be quiet all day. He struggled in many classrooms because he expressed his intelligence kinesthetically and interpersonally. He just wanted to move his body and interact with his environment to acquire his learning, but most skool environments don't cater to these kinds of learners. Needless to say, I got a lot of phone calls and many times I sided with the teachers (even if they weren't always right) because I had been in their shoes. I know how difficult it is to manage twenty-five-plus kids in a classroom and even more difficult when one or two "act a fool."

As a parent, it is important for me to partner with all of my kids' teachers and to work with them to help us achieve our common goal of helping my children be successful academically. When my oldest son was in elementary school, I spent a lot of time in the school because I knew he was a handful and an extra set of eyes and hands in the classroom are always helpful. His third-grade teacher recognized his greatness and embraced our partnership. As a result, he had a fantastic school year with very few discipline issues. To this day, he still says that his third-grade teacher was one of his favorites and she remembers him as a "bright and energetic soul." I will forever be grateful for her ability to see him in a positive way—not as a menace or a nuisance. She may have done that with or without my partnering with her, but it certainly helps for parents to work together *with* teachers (not against them) for students to have an optimized learning experience.

My oldest son's third-grade teacher is not the only one who was able to see beyond his flaws and embrace his unrefined brilliance. Thank you also to his seventh-grade social studies teacher for being completely honest with him and for believing in his potential. A very special thank you to the teachers and administrators who worked with him in the eighth grade to give him grace both inside and outside of the classroom to open doors of opportunity for him.

I have no illusions or delusions about who my children are, and I truly appreciate all of their teachers for working with them and honoring their uniqueness. A lot of this book was inspired by my oldest son's educational journey and the experiences he endured before getting into a learning environment that truly valued him as a person and as a student. I know he was a handful, and it took him many years and many schools to find his way. He finally landed in a very special place with a very special group of people who enveloped him with their love and ignited his inner genius. Being in this space opened the doors for his siblings to experience the same. I am blessed and honored they are now spending their school years in a place where their teachers are equipped to help cultivate their unique gifts. This village is strong and powerful and I am thankful to all of you for wrapping your arms around them when they need love, for cracking the whip when they need discipline, and for believing in them when others may have written them off.

There are so many amazing teachers who have been instrumental in my son's growth and success as he prepares to enter college. I wish there was a way I could thank them all. Like his former history teacher who constantly checks in on him to make sure he's okay after his football games. Or his English teachers who have shown him nothing but love as they worked with him to grow as a writer. I have a special place in my heart for his "other mama" who was his college algebra teacher who knew math was not his strength, but worked with him tirelessly to help him understand the material. One of the things I respect most about her is that although she is a NASA mathematician-turned-teacher, she met him right where he was. She was able to capitalize on his learning style and abilities to get him to a level of understanding that will provide him with a strong foundation as he enters college. She has an incredibly high level of math understanding, but all she asks of her students is their very best, even if it isn't *Hidden Figures*-level math. It is teachers like her, who love and nurture their students through their most challenging academic subjects, that propel the next generation from dreamers to dream achievers.

Thank you to my youngest daughter's math teacher, who dealt with all of her frustrations and mood swings and rebuilt her confidence from the bottom up in not only her math skills but also in herself. Thank you to my oldest daughter's social studies teacher for working his teaching magic in the classroom and transforming her from disliking it to it becoming her favorite academic subject. My gratitude also goes to my oldest daughter's math teacher who was able to help her overcome her learning difference in math so effectively that she moved up two levels. I am also grateful for my youngest son's first, second, and third-grade teachers who created an experience so exceptional that he and his friends cried because they didn't want it to end.

This list is not exhaustive—I could go on and on with thanksgiving for the people who pour their all into my own children. Writing this chapter was the most difficult for me because I have been a student, teacher, and administrator, and I am also a parent. I understand the calling to teach, but I also know how difficult, stressful, and taxing this job is. I know the rewards are not typically monetary, but they are incredibly beneficial, and they live on and on . . . forever. Teachers, I hope you know just how much you are appreciated, even if you don't hear it directly from your students. There are not enough pages in this book to thank teachers for all they do, but I hope my words can serve as a small token of my appreciation and reflect the grateful hearts of so many others who have been positively impacted by the work of teachers in their lives. So, if you are a teacher, keep doing what you do—we love and appreciate you!

CHAPTER 7
PARENTS R . . .

The powerhouse of education. However, many parents have no idea of the power they possess—or how to use it. This chapter will explore the ways parents can take back their power to ensure that no matter how skoolz and skool systems operate, their children can have the best educational experience possible.

When I started out as an educator, I didn't have any children of my own. I didn't know what it was like to be a parent or to know another human being in such a deeply personal and intimate way, but my students were my "babies." It was important for me to get to know them and have an understanding of what motivated them and how they learned best. Although there were many of them (I taught six classes per day with anywhere from twenty-four to thirty-three kids per class), I did my best to develop relationships with them and get to know them. However, there are few relationships deeper and more complex than that of parent and child. People shift their focus when they become parents. The emphasis pivots from self to others and, in particular, that focus is on the lives of the little human(s) that have been entrusted to them. When you are a parent, there is an instinct to not only love and nurture, but also to correct and protect, that kicks in differently. There are some people who do not have children but have a special gifting or calling to work with them. These people are innately nurturing, loving, and have a special place in their hearts for young folks. These are the characteristics good teachers have, and although I recall wanting to be extra protective of children even before I had my own, I learned very quickly that parenting your own children is a very different beast.

Parenting, for some, comes at a very young age—an age in which people feel they grow up with their children. For others it comes when they are much older and "seasoned" in the game of life; and still others, right in between. There is no right or wrong time to become a parent and no matter how old or young, rich or poor, or what level of educational attainment a parent may have, *all* parents make mistakes! One of the greatest mistakes I have witnessed is for parents to give their power to skoolz and skool systems. It has been my observation that this power is often given up more by parents who are younger or lack higher levels of education. However, any parent who may not know as much about education as they would like, regardless of their educational or socioeconomic status, can fall prey to this powerlessness which is a tragedy. Unfortunately, some skoolz exploit these parents and further disarm them by using what they don't know about education against them.

When my oldest son was in kindergarten, he attended a magnet elementary school that was at least 98 percent children of color and 53 percent of the student body were considered economically disadvantaged—yet whenever there was a PTA meeting, it was standing room only. If you didn't arrive at the school at least ten minutes prior to the start of the meeting, you would not be able to find a parking space and would find yourself walking from a block away just to get to the meeting. The same rang true for me when I was a student. My elementary school was predominantly Black and so was the teacher population, however on PTA nights, both teachers and parents/families showed up in full force, building community and networking with one another. Needless to say, when our family moved from Georgia to Minnesota and I was the only Black parent in attendance for the first PTA meeting I attended, I was baffled. My son's new school was more than 60 percent students of color, yet when I drove into the parking lot, it was so empty I thought I had gotten the schedule mixed up and showed up on the wrong night. There were only eight parking spaces up front and the lot was typically full, but on that night, there was actually a space to park, which surprised me. I was even more confused when I walked into the meeting and I was the only Black parent in attendance.

I was curious and wanted to know more. At the time, I did not have a full-time job, so I had some time on my hands to do a little investigating. I talked with the principal and created a survey designed to measure parents' attitudes about their school involvement. Questions from that survey are as follows:

Dear Parents,

In effort to help serve all of our North Park families more effectively, we have created a short survey to learn more about you. Please fill it out and return inside your child's Thursday Folder. Thank you for your time.

1.) In your opinion, are you involved in your child's education? If yes, in what ways are you involved? (Check all that apply)

Helping with homework

Volunteering at school

Participating in PTA

Frequent communication with your child's teacher

Other _____

2.) What are some ways the North Park staff, teachers, and parent volunteers can help you to be more involved with your child's education?

Homework help/hotline

Providing childcare for meetings

Providing transportation for meetings

Assistance with communication/language barriers

Other _____

3.) What are the greatest challenges you face in being involved with your child's education?

Transportation

Communication/Language Barriers

Childcare issues

Work schedule

School environment

Other _____

4.) How many days of work do you miss (if any) per year for your child's behavior/academic reasons?

_____

5.) What is your nationality/ethnicity?

_____

6.) How do you identify your child's nationality/ethnicity?

_____

Please provide us with your contact information:

_____

_____

_____

Name:

_____

Child(ren)'s names/grades:

_____

_____

_____

_____

Phone Number:

_____

Email Address:

_____

Once the surveys were completed, I reached out to African American families. Please note that I was especially interested in the African American/Black perspective because it is this population that often gets labeled as not being involved in their children's education. I moved from a predominantly Black community with what I perceived to be a very involved parent community (at least by way of attending PTA meetings) to a community in which around 35 percent to 40 percent of the student population was African American/Black and I was the only one in attendance to the PTA meetings.

I distinctly remember a conversation with one of the fathers who gave me a perspective that truly opened my eyes. When I asked him if he ever came to meetings or even up to the school to do classroom observations, he told me he was not comfortable. I was actually surprised and wanted to learn more. Upon further elaboration, he told me that he had limited education and graduated with a GED, so he didn't feel comfortable in the presence of the teachers and administrators, who had considerably more formal education than he did. As I listened to what he was saying, it hit me like a brick that even as a Black woman, I had been operating from a place of privilege throughout my educational journey, during the survey process, and basically my entire life. My grandmother and great-aunts were all educators and had graduated college. My father had a master's degree and spent forty years teaching and coaching high school students. I had a master's degree, taught school, and had an enjoyable K–12 educational experience, and here I was questioning this father's lack of physical presence within a school environment. It was mind-blowing, and I was instantly embarrassed by my ignorance. Wow! Talk about privilege—my educational background and social upbringing prevented me from ever thinking about this perspective prior to this conversation.

I wanted to digest this thought further, but more importantly, I wanted to empower him in that moment to help him understand how important his physical presence was in the schools his children attended. I told him that despite the levels of formal education and professional experience of the teachers who worked with his children daily, he and, of course, his children's mother are the most knowledgeable about them. Nobody outside of him and their mother had gotten the opportunity to get to know his children in ways they did. He knew their likes and dislikes, their interests, favorite toys, songs, and pastimes, and what got them to respond in different ways. I had to convince him of the importance of his presence in the schools. If his job and lifestyle would allow him the opportunity to take time to come to his children's school/classroom, he could observe how his children interacted with school personnel so teachers could communicate with him firsthand about how his children were progressing, both academically and personally. (Ironically, this would be true of me a year later, when my oldest child's teacher told me that coming into his classroom helped her interact with him more effectively.)

When I stepped back from that conversation, it occurred to me that if *he* felt this way, there had to be many others who also shared those same sentiments. All those years, I had been operating in oblivion, thinking that parents who weren't "visibly involved" in their children's education may be too busy, lacked childcare, or just weren't interested. It had never crossed my mind that a parent may feel uneasy, distressed, or even traumatized in the presence of school personnel. This made me reconsider how I defined parent involvement and made me wonder how many of these parents may be viewed negatively by skool personnel and how that negative view impacts the education of their children.

As I continued to make phone calls to other families, I learned so much about the thoughts and mindsets of the parents I spoke to. Moving to Minnesota and having these conversations helped me see my own privilege and made me consider a perspective I had never thought of. I learned that the power my own parents and I possessed and wielded so well in educational environments is something we all have, but many don't necessarily know how to tap into or maximize it in a way that yields the results we desire.

This experience helped me learn that some people are actually intimidated by teachers and administrators and sometimes the skool environment in general. Everybody didn't have pleasant experiences with skoolz—making good grades, rarely getting in serious trouble, and having a hunky-dory good time—so, naturally, there may be some ill feelings and, in some cases, trauma related to school that carry over into their adulthood. I once saw a video where the presenter used "your child's teacher" in the same category as police officers and medical professionals, and how those feelings of inferiority affect the ability of people to utilize their own personal power with them. These were his words:

> *"We perceive ourselves to be beneath them, we perceive ourselves in the position of 'I'm the one that's selling something' or 'I'm the one that wants something' so the other person has the advantage, they have the leverage. There are times in our lives when we are having conversations with people and they know more than we do, or they are in this perceived superior position to us and it makes you feel kinda like you're deferring to them, like they're the boss . . . But in this situation, you need to feel like you are the PhD of the universe! YOU are the medical doctor, YOU are the principal of the school, YOU are the bossiest boss-boss-boss of the product, so YOU need to have the authority to lead the conversation . . ."*

Although I do not remember the name of the speaker or the source of the video, these words couldn't be truer when parents consider their relationships with teachers/school administrators and the authority they have when it comes to their children. Unfortunately, feeling powerful can be difficult for parents who don't feel comfortable in educational environments. All the acronyms, abbreviations, and lingo associated with schools and school systems are not only sometimes difficult to decipher and understand, but are also different depending upon where you're located, not to mention all the norms and rules that differ from place to place. As a parent of four, I know how difficult it can be just to keep up with homework assignments and make sure that kids have a decent breakfast before they leave for school, much less trying to figure out all the other pieces that are a part of their educational puzzle. Learning all of the vocabulary and regulations associated with each child's educational experience is a daunting task, but it is my hope that I can help. In this chapter, we will examine ways to navigate through the aftermath of pandemics, the intricacies of data, the rigidity of systems, and the "ridicula of curricula" in order to help you feel most empowered throughout your child's academic journey.

As we explore these areas, I would like to introduce what I call the

"Trifecta of Parent Power" that parents have over their child's education experience—the "Power of Presence," the "Power of Participation," and the "Power of Persuasion." Although each of these powers is effective when implemented individually, when combined, this trifecta of powers is astronomical in its impact on a child throughout their educational journey.

THE POWER OF PRESENCE

From the beginning of first grade up until the second half of his second-grade year, I homeschooled my oldest son using the K–12 online curriculum. It was rigorous, and there were many power struggles between him and me during those school days, but what I learned most about him during that time was his need for social interaction with peers. So, when our family made the move from Georgia to Minnesota and I dropped him off at his new school for the first time, it was one of the happiest days of both of our lives!

Although he was going to be in a traditional school environment, I still wanted to remain involved. I knew that historically, he was quite an "active" child in the classroom and although he was no longer being homeschooled, he needed to know I was never too far away. I would go to PTA meetings, volunteer in the classroom and/or for events taking place at the school, and became pretty well known there. I would bring my younger children with me and the school community showered us with support and love. Our family was part of their family and the school felt more like a second home, which helped with our transition to a new place.

When my son went to third grade, my oldest daughter started kindergarten, and my involvement increased. There were many days I would spend time in the classroom and serve as an unofficial "Classroom Mom" for not just my own son, but for the other students in his class as well. My son had a great third-grade year and really loved his teacher, "Ms. B," who I also thought was phenomenal. Despite my son's occasional "over activeness," Ms. B really interacted well with him, and she rarely had behavior issues with him.

Near the end of the year, "Ms. B" pulled me aside and told me she appreciated my presence in her classroom during the year. She said it was my interactions with my son that helped her connect with him in ways that he would positively respond to when he was behaving in ways not conducive to the learning environment. I never knew it at the time, but I had been modeling my motherly behavior to her, which helped her more effectively engage with my son and some of her other students. As a Black mother of four, I was able to help a young, single white woman with no children of her own to better connect with students who had a different background and upbringing—just by being in the room. Even though I had not intentionally set out to do this, I learned that the Power of Presence is very real and makes a huge difference—even when we don't know it is happening.

One of the best examples of the Power of Presence I've ever heard of took place at a high school in Shreveport, Louisiana, where the presence of a group of fathers not only stopped violent behaviors, but has shifted the entire school culture for the better. At Southwood High School, a rash of fights broke out over a period of three consecutive days, leading to the arrest of twenty-three students. A group of fathers recognized this as a problem that could be easily solved just by "showing up"—and it worked! About forty fathers of Southwood High School students came to the school every day, greeting kids at the door and in the hallways, encouraging kids to get to class on time, and cracking "dad jokes." They don't have guns at their hips and they don't use physical force to get kids to do what they are supposed to do—they just make their presence known. Once they started this, the fighting and violence at the school stopped.

You can tell by the footage of them throughout the school that they are not only having a great time in the presence of the students and each other, but that the students appreciate them being there. The interview that the men had with CBS News was short, but effectively conveyed the incredible impact of the Power of Presence—no fancy degrees or classes necessary.

In the interview, dads and students were asked about the impact and influence of the dads while they were on campus. The dads emphasized that as parents, they were the best people to help transform the negative behaviors of the students. The students reciprocated their sentiments by expressing how powerful it is just for them to be in the hallways, share dad jokes, or to just "give a look." To view the video, please visit the KSLA website (https://www.ksla.com) and enter "Dads on Duty" in the search field, or find it on YouTube at: https://www.youtube.com/watch?v=OdPaqt6RY_Q

You may learn about their work and donate to their mission by visiting http://www.dadsondutyusa.org/

THE POWER OF PARTICIPATION

Participation, though it involves presence, takes it a step further by not just "being there," but also "doing something." The Power of Participation includes helping with homework, reading to your child's class, or maybe even participating in foot races with kids on field day. This kind of power is action that creates and/or inspires action in others. Kids love this type of power and though they may not ever say anything, the Power of Participation serves as a major source of inspiration. There is something special that lights up in a kid when their coach can do a backflip for winning a championship or their teacher can do the latest TikTok dance—parents are no different. They don't have to work to try to win the "Cool Parent Award" with physical feats—they just have to *do* something and they don't have to have tons of education to do so.

One of my friends told me that she learned about percentages from her mom, who secretly taught her to calculate them in her head. She told me that every Saturday, they would do shopping of some sort, either for groceries, clothes, shoes, or other needs and wants.

Whenever there was a sale, she would ask how much the total cost would be once the percentage was applied. If grapes were 40 percent off of a two-dollar bag, she would need to calculate that they were discounted by eighty cents and the price would be $1.20. If shoes were one-third off the lowest marked price, she would have to figure it out and let her mother know. She told me this occurred all throughout her childhood and over time she became very good at calculating percentages and fractions. Once she got older, her mother confessed to her that she never knew the answers but wanted her to figure out the projected totals so it would help her know how much she would have to pay at the checkout counter.

This is the perfect example of the Power of Participation and its impact on a child's thought processes and learning experiences. By taking her daughter to the store every Saturday (doing something) and requiring her daughter to work out the problems in her head, my friend's mother helped her develop a skill she mastered and has been able to use throughout her lifetime.

The pandemic forced many parents to spend more time with their children than they ever have. Shutting down schools and restricting access to public places meant that parents instantly became their children's teachers and mentors, which was a welcome change for some, but an overwhelming burden to others. Some families had all the resources and knowledge necessary to quickly transform their homes into classrooms or learning pods, but others lacked home internet access, breakfast and lunch options, and computers for their children to use. Regardless of what end of the spectrum a family was on, the common thread was that they had the opportunity to "do" more with their children and learn more about their academic needs than before. Parents learned firsthand of their children's struggles with their times tables or difficulty with reading comprehension. It's possible that they also got to witness more of their children's artistic or athletic talents. As terrible as it was, the pandemic presented the opportunity to help parents gain a more in-depth understanding of their children. During this time, they were able to get insights into their children's interests and abilities they may not have known otherwise. This was a period in which many parents had the opportunity to exert the Power of Participation in ways they had not previously done.

In addition to working directly with children, the Power of Participation can also be accomplished through joining groups such as PTA organizations, volunteering in schools, and getting involved in political arenas to show support and make a change in children's educational lives. Sometimes, these more formal methods of participation are complicated to navigate, but there are ways to make your entrance into these arenas a little less taxing and even if someone is new to this form of participation, it is not as difficult as one may imagine.

Schools, as I must continue to emphasize, are nothing without people to make them what they are. In so many ways, it is the schools whose parents are most involved through the Power of Participation that have some of the most successful student populations. Parents are the powerhouse not only because of their actual participation but also because those who exert the Power of Participation through school and system involvement often also understand their own Power of Presence and use their Power of Persuasion to make things happen and influence the lives of their own and other children. I realize some parental organizations might be frowned upon and maybe even laughed at, because of the stereotypical and clique-ish image they sometimes present, but they provide valuable opportunities to obtain information, express ideas, and build influence. This is also a chance for parents to become a part of a group that provides support, guidance, and resources for a wide range of educational situations.

The key piece to connecting to bigger organizations is to seek out leadership to find out where help is needed most. Sometimes they are looking to increase membership, or volunteers for the upcoming fundraiser. Usually, a person's willingness to lend a hand goes a long way in building rapport and getting your foot in the door. Simple tasks such as making phone calls, working at a table or booth, or stuffing envelopes to mail letters are ways to lend a helping hand and start connecting. I remember one of the biggest needs for the PTA at my daughters' school was sorting, counting, and bagging the Box Tops for Education coupons that parents brought in. The funding that came from Box Tops was substantial and the need for extra counting hands was significant. These types of tasks are perfect for those who would prefer not to be in the spotlight but still want to contribute in a meaningful way. The efforts of those who lend help in this way are appreciated by school personnel and don't go unnoticed.

If you would like to take your Power of Participation to an even larger "organized" scale; going to school board meetings, or running for office are options that work to benefit your children, though perhaps at the expense of time with them. Please keep this in mind if you are interested in serving in this way, you will likely trade out much of your personal time for public time—school board members are public servants who spend a lot of time in meetings and "serving the people." It is the main reason that, for all of the times people have asked me to run for city council or school board, I have kindly declined. For me, it is much more important to effect change either directly or at the school level, so I may protect the time I have with my children while they are still young.

THE POWER OF PERSUASION

The Power of Persuasion works in two ways—persuading those who influence your child or children and persuading your child directly. Persuading those who are working with your child/children is important and can certainly open doors that may otherwise be closed. This can be done through the Power of Presence and the Power of Participation. Sometimes it's how you show up that makes the difference in whether your child gains access to certain opportunities. Being present and participating makes it much easier to "persuade" others who work with your children. The Power of Persuasion is often a byproduct of the Power of Presence and the Power of Participation.

Persuasion can come forth as a result of presence and participation, but it often comes through in the messages you share with your child and how those messages are conveyed, either verbally or nonverbally. With all of the other obvious factors that play a role in student success—academic content/curriculum, resources, teacher influence, etc.—the Power of Persuasion is often overlooked. So many students internalize this power and make decisions—both good and bad—because of the impact that it has on their thoughts and belief systems. Persuasion is defined as "a deep conviction or belief" (www.dictionary.com) or "communication intended to induce belief or action" (www.rhymezone.com). The reason why this is an important aspect to focus on is because it is the very first power a child learns from their parents, and those thoughts and beliefs help shape how they approach their own education and the decisions they make in their lives.

Whether parents are consciously aware of it or not, they are their child's very first teacher and influencer in life. The first voice heard by them in the womb is that of their mother's, with whoever is around the mother most running a close second. Babies start to gain an understanding of the world around them as early as their gestational period in the womb. Hearing is one of the first fully developed senses—allowing fetuses to hear in utero. Something as simple as whether a mother listens to calming classical music or clanging chords of chaos can have an effect on a baby's development. Even if a parent is not an educational expert, he or she can take important steps in their child's early development and path to higher levels of learning by playing music, reading books, or even talking to the growing fetus in a way that is loving and supportive. As I mentioned in a previous chapter, no human being has to be "taught to learn"—it is an automatic response and everything we say and do is learned by babies as they take in the world around them. Their parents' (or caregivers') Power of Persuasion has a strong impact on their educational mindset and perspectives toward school and themselves.

When we teach our children the alphabet, point to different colors, and teach them the names of people, places, and things, we use our Power of Persuasion to start their process of learning more about the world around them. My mother proved this with my ability to communicate as a child and how she taught me to communicate with my children. She told me she never spoke "baby talk" (goo-goo, ga-ga) to my brother and me, but would always speak in complete sentences with us, so we had quite a command of the English language, even at a young age. I did the same with my own children, and by the time they started school, their vocabulary was far beyond the average 2,600-word vocabulary of a five-year-old. It always makes me smile to hear them use words that many of their peers wouldn't even imagine using at their young ages. That strong foundation of communication came simply from being intentional about the vocabulary they learned from me and my husband when they were in the womb and while they were babies.

One of my greatest pet peeves is hearing parents curse at their young children, and while I have my own potty-mouth moments, cursing at small children is something I am strongly against. Ensuring we shield their young minds against strong derogatory language helps protect them from early trauma and maintains their innocence. I remember being in a store with a lady who had been cursing at her young son, who couldn't have been more than about two years old. She continued to refer to him as "bad," and I kindly told her that he's not "bad," but instead "curious" and "active." I told her that children often manifest behaviors that mirror their labels, which could lead a child who's not really bad to end up carrying out "bad behaviors." No child is "bad" at their core but, unfortunately, sometimes the stresses of life will cause parents to project that a child is bad because they struggle to manage the curiosities and excessive energy their children possess.

As they grow and learn, children's minds are also molded from "messages" that are fed to them. They not only take in what you say, but they are also influenced by what you don't say and how you respond to your environment. Babies and children are very perceptive and can pick up thoughts and ideas, whether we intend for them to or not. When it comes to preparing our children for the school environment, the messages shared with children by their parents have a direct impact on how they behave and perceive their teachers, classrooms, and peers. Have you heard a parent tell a child, "If a teacher doesn't let you go to the bathroom, just get up and go anyway"? Or a child say "My mama said, 'You betta not put your hands on me!'"? In what context are these messages presented to children? What kind of tone goes along with those messages? The ways in which parents deliver these messages to their children makes a huge impact on the outlook of their educational experiences.

Depending upon how these directives are presented to a child, it can cause them to develop unnecessary negative viewpoints about schools and teachers before they even step foot in a classroom. This is an example of how the Power of Persuasion can be used to plant negative ideals and beliefs in children about teachers and classrooms, even if there is no intent to do so. Sometimes these and other similar messages are spoken with defensive overtones, so children go into schools vigilant and ready for a teacher to say or do something sideways just because they want to be ready for the clapback. I can't speak for each and every teacher, but most teachers are not trying to be malicious when working with children and their bodily needs. Sometimes circumstances are such that one bathroom break could lead to a domino effect of many, so they need their students to hold on for just a bit to maintain a conducive learning environment. And, let's be honest, sometimes the students are being just plain defiant and are trying to find a way out of the classroom under the guise of a bursting bladder. Kids are highly intelligent (and sometimes manipulative) beings who use their own Power of Persuasion to create conflict between teachers and parents. The messages delivered through the Power of Persuasion in situations like this could lead children to think teachers and administrators are "out to get them," or that they can get away with doing whatever they want, causing them to act out in ways that create problems for themselves and others. By contrast, parents who use the Power of Persuasion with their children in positive ways while partnering with teachers and administrators can influence them to achieve greater levels of success.

(As a side note: I definitely believe the Power of Persuasion should be used to help children protect themselves and trust their instincts when things may not be right. So, when speaking with children about being able to go to the bathroom or being touched inappropriately, it is important for them to learn to communicate effectively with the adults they are interacting with and know when and whom to tell when they feel they are being harmed.)

There are some instances in which teachers are in the wrong and children have to advocate for themselves. Teachers don't know it all, and the classroom should be a place in which children should feel free to respectfully challenge academic rhetoric that over time has been widely accepted as truth, but is not completely factual. If you are a parent who uses your Power of Persuasion to teach your child or children to think outside of the (classroom) box and provide them with more in-depth wisdom than what is often taught in their schools, then I wholeheartedly commend you and encourage you to do more of it. I think children, especially children of color, should never be afraid to expose some of the lies about their history told in schools, and while some schools are working toward antiracism and a more equitable experience for their student population, many are not, and in general have quite a way to go in their Diversity Equity and Inclusion (DEI) efforts. (*Unfortunately, DEI and culturally competent teaching and learning efforts have been villainized in many skoolz. However, the whitewashing of curriculum and censoring the most brutal and embarrassing parts of American history is a step backward in advancing the education of all of our children.*)

In many ways, your tone and body language are just as powerful in persuasion as the words you speak. When parents are communicating about education and to educators, a positive attitude goes a long way in how children feel about their school experiences. If they feel you are supportive and enthusiastic about school, kids often follow suit and work hard to ensure they approach their educational experiences with zeal, especially when they are younger. But, if they are constantly exposed to messages painted with images of hostile environments that require a verbal or physical altercation, their view of school is tainted. It is from this tainted view that negative classroom behaviors and low achievement can be conceived.

The Power of Persuasion may also have good intentions that are misinterpreted by those receiving the messages being shared. Even when parents' messages are meant for good, it's important to further clarify what we mean and have discussions with our kids surrounding our persuasive messages so they have a full understanding of what we are really trying to say. Sometimes our words are not always translated in the minds of our children the way we want them to. This is especially true for kids who are like I was—stubborn, bullheaded, and thought I knew everything (like many young people). As a teenager, I had my own idea of what the world was like and I interpreted my parents' advice in a way I thought was best for me in my immature teenage mind, but that wasn't necessarily ideal for my future self.

Throughout my young life, my parents used their power of persuasion to feed my confidence and push me in the right direction. They were great messages and they ultimately led me on a well-educated path. However, there are two of those messages I misconstrued in my young mind, and by doing so, I hindered myself from achieving my goals and aspirations. Those two persuasive messages are as follows:

Message 1: My mom told me, "You *will* graduate from high school and you *will* graduate from college. Whatever you do beyond that is on you."

My mother's intention: To hold me to a high standard of academic excellence and encourage me to remain focused so I could achieve the goals of a high school diploma and a college degree. A high school education was just the beginning and I needed to continue to aim high and pursue greater academic goals.

My interpretation: *A college education is my only route to a successful life and if I stray from this path to pursue a trade, entrepreneurship, or creative ventures without a college degree, I am doomed to failure. As long as I get a college degree, I will be able to achieve anything. That piece of paper is the gateway to my success in life.*

Message 2: My dad told me, "If you graduate from a "good school" with a great reputation, you can do whatever you want to do."

My father's intention: To let me know a reputable degree would open doors of opportunity.

My interpretation: *All I need to do is cross the stage and obtain the degree and it will be enough for me to go anywhere and do anything I want to do. The name on the degree is all I need to write my ticket to success, and I don't have to do anything else because by just graduating I will have done enough. Chill through college—party, hang out, do the bare minimum, and don't get involved in campus activities—and I'll be all right. The name of the school on my degree is powerful enough to get me anywhere I want to go.*

Although my parents intended these messages to further propel my desire to excel, *I* used it as an excuse to abandon it altogether. My interpretation of these two messages created the perfect storm of self-limiting behaviors and beliefs that struck down my driving force like lightning and rained on my overconfident parade. I finished both high school and college and earned my degree from big school/good reputation. The dignitaries called my name and I proudly walked across the stage to receive this coveted piece of paper written in fancy letters, and when I got it, I realized that's all it was. There was no fabulous job offer with a large salary wrapped inside—it was just a fancy piece of paper.

It was in this moment that I learned a very humbling message—the school doesn't make the people; the *people* make the school. It's the *people* at the school who have the networks and power to open doors of opportunities. It's the *people* at the school who have the ability to recognize the potential in others and connect them to jobs and careers. The "good school" with great reputation I attended is not a "smart school," it just attracts smart *people*, who have done and continue to do smart things that have helped build the smart reputation it has. The same is true for *any* school with a great reputation. The excellent reputation schools have doesn't come from the school itself, but instead from the excellence of the people who go and went to school there, who teach and taught there, and who are affiliated with those people. Big schools with great reputations never had the power to "make me" who I am—*I* am the one who possessed the power to take what I learned from the amazing people there to do and become "whatever I wanted." Unfortunately, I gave away my power to the school, thinking the school would make me into who I needed to be without me having to do the work to achieve my goals.

Because of my own misinterpretation of my parents' messages, all of the hard work I put in to serve in leadership positions, make good grades, and score high on tests in high school ended once I stepped foot on my college campus. It never occurred to me that all the work I needed to accomplish to obtain the scholarships and get accepted to college was the same work I needed to put into my college experience if I wanted the same or a similar result when I graduated with my undergraduate degree. I naively believed all I needed to do was graduate and the world would be my oyster. I naively believed I could hang out and do just enough to get by in my classes and the name of the school alone would carry me to the promised land. I went on interview after interview and even the jobs I thought would be given to me left me without offers. I wanted to get a job that, in my mind, "matched" with my new degree, but I was not successful. I failed miserably at getting a great job that promised the high pay I thought would come along with my big-school-with-great-reputation degree. Deep down I felt like I had failed myself and my parents.

All around me, the people I knew were graduating from college and getting high-paying jobs in career fields that matched their majors and all I had was the same job I had before I graduated. The Power of Persuasion framed my thinking about college and for a long time, I was resentful of my college and the education I received there when *I* was the one that didn't take full advantage of my experience. It was all on me the whole time and I just didn't know it. I allowed the messages I had received about college to resonate with me in a way that caused me to become complacent. I thought all I had to do was make it to the finish line with the degree in my hand and miraculously all of the job opportunities and career pathways would appear at my doorstep. But they didn't.

Through my green envy-colored lenses and resentment, I couldn't see that the others who were doing well made the best of their academic, social, and extracurricular opportunities when they were completing their undergraduate degrees, and the world was indeed their oyster once they graduated. They didn't all graduate with the highest grades or academic honors, but they were involved in clubs, sororities and fraternities, and other campus activities that enriched their college experiences. They were rewarded with high-paying jobs and careers that allowed them to fast-track professionally.

I share these stories so parents take the time to replay their own messages in their head, reflect on how they may be misinterpreted, and reframe those messages if necessary. Are we projecting our own fears, concerns, or limiting beliefs on our kids through our Power of Persuasion? Do our kids understand the perspectives we bring when we share our advice? Is there another person who could enhance our messages or share a different viewpoint?

Ensuring your children have other highly intelligent, wise people to be a part of their village is so important. My parents were the only adult perspective I knew and trusted. There was no other person—coach, mentor, faculty member, or guide—that helped me navigate my college years, so there were gaps in my understanding of the world. As a parent, it is important to recognize your flaws and limitations and admit you don't know it all. Make sure your kids know you don't have all the answers and that it's good to hear from other perspectives when making decisions or just going through their day-to-day lives.

When there are instances in which I am limited in my understanding or expertise, I do my best to defer to the experts. Although I was a college athlete, the recruiting process has changed significantly since the time I started school—especially for football, which is a sport I did not participate in. So, from the time my son decided he wanted to pursue football, not just as a recreational sport/activity, but ultimately as a profession, I began to lean on my brother for help. Why? Because, for the past twenty years, he has been helping young men get full scholarships to play football in college and beyond. I trust the process and the expert in this instance, and it has led to incredible success for my son. Although I was a teacher and took the special needs course required to become a certified educator, when my daughter was diagnosed with a learning difference, I reached out to teachers and advisers who could provide me with knowledge and refer me to resources to help her become academically successful. As parents, we often want to step in and give our "two cents," but there are many teachers, coaches, mentors, and others in our village who not only care about our children, but also have the expertise that will get them where they need and want to be.

Even if you don't have a well-established friend group who can share their insights or family members who have journeyed the same path our children want to pursue, there are many ways they can be enriched and advised. We live in a day and age in which we can be intentional in our parenting about how to guide our kids through life. With the expansion of the internet, social media outlets, and the overall globalization of access to information, there are many ways to get what you need to help your child in all areas of their lives, even if you don't have a background or expertise in those areas.

Most importantly, please be careful not to use your Power of Persuasion to get your kids to "follow in your footsteps" or carry on a real or imagined legacy you have built unless it is truly designed for them. Far too many times, I have seen parents establish expectations of their children based on themselves and what they loved or were good at without taking into account what their children deem most important. Be honest with yourself about your children—who they are now and who they want to be. Maybe your kid really isn't a good athlete although you have trophies and medals to boast about. Or maybe you graduated with honors and school came easy to you, but psychological testing has revealed that your child has a learning difference and is struggling to read or do math. These are realities that may be difficult for you to accept, but it's important for parents to really get to know their children and use the Power of Persuasion to ultimately allow their children to grow and feel free to make decisions that work best for them. Stop forcing your son to play baseball if he doesn't like sports and would rather spend his time drawing. Listen to your daughter when she tells you she likes robots and engineering but you're pushing her to do competitive cheer.

At the end of the day, most kids just want to please their parents and will sometimes go along blindly to please them, even if they are miserable. It breaks my heart to see kids reluctantly playing a sport or being forced to participate in activities or being forced to sit out from doing what they really want to do just because their parents want (or don't want) them to. Kids work hard to try to fit into the molds their parents create for them and the extra pressure of trying to meet their parents' expectations could be life-altering and breed resentment and regret. Use the Power of Presence and the Power of Participation to really get to know who your children are, and the Power of Persuasion to encourage them to be their best selves in *their* lane—not yours. Have high expectations of your children and expose them to a variety of different exploits, but also listen to them, observe their mannerisms, and be supportive of *their* interests and skill sets. This is where the powers of Presence, Participation, and Persuasion merge, harnessing the force that your parental powerhouse needs for you to propel your children beyond their highest potential and into their purpose-filled destinies.

CHAPTER 8
STUDENTS R . . .

The *why*.

In recent years, we hear many entrepreneurs, mentors, and other trusted advisers tell people to identify their "why." The "why" is the reason you want to lose weight, make more money, or discover your passion. The "why" is what keeps us going when times get rough and we want to give up on our paths to our goals. Without the "why," whatever we pursue is in vain. In the world of education, no matter how great the facilities, effective the curriculum, or dynamic the teachers, if the students are not the "why," then it is all pointless. Students are the foundation and their well-being and success should be the reason why educational systems exist in the first place. Unfortunately, though, the many components required to establish and maintain educational systems—data, curricula, mandates, and structures—have become the focus, leaving students in the background. The pandemic exposed how much the focus has shifted away from the students and onto the system. It is now time to reestablish the foundation and focus on the students for whom the systems were designed in the first place.

Students are (or should be) at the very core of all of the decisions that schools make. Yet, in far too many instances, schools neglect this most important piece of the puzzle. In recent years, I have noticed that there is an increase in student input through surveys and student-centered learning. However, I don't know that enough efforts are being put forth to ensure the needs of our most important (and vulnerable) stakeholders are being met. Am I saying we should just give children *all* the say in their education? Absolutely not! If we left it up to them, they might say it would suffice them to learn all they need to know from Minecraft, Roblox, Fortnite, YouTube videos, TikTok, and Instagram. As adults, we have the prudence and wisdom to know that this will not allow them to fully realize their potential and gain the knowledge they need to prepare for college and career paths in their futures (although there is much that can be learned from these platforms). However, we definitely need to accept that this is their world—filled with technology, driven by a myriad of media sources that as children many of us couldn't even dream of. How do we take the knowledge they need to know and use their modern media as the vehicle to drive it into their minds and prepare them for their future?

We also need to understand that after four to six months of being locked down in their homes for quarantining and sheltering in place, followed by more than a year of remote and/or hybrid learning models, it was a disservice for students to go back to school as normal, and we are now seeing how detrimental it was. Children and young people are incredibly perceptive and insightful and sometimes prophetic. About six months before the pandemic forced us to conduct school and work from home, my youngest son, who was only four at the time, put his wishes out into the atmosphere. There were many mornings in which he cried, kicked, and screamed, completely resisting the bus ride he wanted to experience so badly the summer before. He told me, "Mommy, I don't have to go to school. I can just stay at home and do ABCMouse.com." The popular online learning platform for younger children is filled with songs, videos, and fun games that have helped many children learn foundational academic concepts. I rationalized to myself that while this made sense to me, it would not allow me to continue to work my job because I would have to quit to stay home with him. Although I completely agreed with him, I knew I was restricted by my own teaching obligations and we would have to continue to have to drag him down the street to the bus stop until the end of the school year. Covid-19 put an end to those shenanigans much more quickly than any of us expected, and here I was, faced with the opportunity to allow him to do ABCMouse.com to finish out his pre-K school year.

I first saw a glimpse into the power of learning from media with my oldest daughter. My oldest son forced me into early retirement from pre-K homeschooling, so I had totally given up on the idea of using flashcards, puzzles, and games with the rest of my kids. They played freely with whatever toys they had as PBS Kids ran on the TV in the background. Yes, I know I am a teacher, and yes, I know that screen time should be limited, blah-blah-blah, but I figured they needed to get their ABCs and 123s from somewhere because I didn't have the patience to sit down with them and teach it. So, although my method was lazy, I learned how genius it was when my sixteen-month-old daughter reached for a bottle of nail polish, but ended up accidentally spilling it all across her toes and the top of her foot. Instead of making a bigger mess right there in the kitchen, I decided to take her to the back porch to clean it up. As I was rubbing nail polish remover on her feet with a napkin, she started pointing at the letters on the welcome mat.

"W," she called out, with no prompting from me. I immediately froze in my tracks and began to look around as though perhaps there may be some mystical "Letter Fairy" floating around telling her what to say.

"E," she continued on. By now, I was really in shock. I did not ever recall sitting down with her with flashcards, puzzles, games, or any such thing to teach her these letters, yet here she was, correctly identifying them with no prodding of my own. At this point, I had to ask, with hesitation, "Do you know your letters?" She nodded shyly and I asked her to identify the other letters on the mat. She continued to correctly identify them, and it finally struck me that somewhere between the PBS Kids shows *Word World*, *Super Why!*, and *Martha*

Speaks, she had learned the letters of the alphabet. I was impressed and happily satisfied to know that these TV shows actually worked. In the book *The Tipping Point*, Malcolm Gladwell noted that Finland is regarded as the most highly literate country in the world, although kids there don't start school until they are seven years old. He goes on to say that they watch TV with subtitles, which contributes to their ability to read. When this incident occurred with my daughter, I thought about this concept and realized it actually may have some validity with all learning concepts, but didn't revisit the idea until many years later, after I had been exposed to the concepts of individualized and student-centered learning.

I was living in the state of Minnesota (known for their progressive nature and innovation in the area of education) when I first formally learned about individualized and student-centered learning. By this time, I had been involved in organizations, and had begun establishing myself as a parent advocate for education. I don't think my youngest son was even a year old yet and we were invited to a neighbor's house for lunch. As they were preparing to serve the meal, the kids played and their youngest son brought out some Hot Wheels and Matchbox cars for my baby boy to play with. There had to be no less than one hundred cars in the container and when he saw them, his face lit up with joy in a way I had never seen before. He was known for saying "Eat-Eat" because whenever it was time to eat, he was ready and quickly abandoned whatever he was doing to get to his meal, but this time he was different. It was as if he were bound by his fascination with these cars and I watched as he took them out of the container and strategically placed them all over their back porch. He examined each one of them, meticulously as a medical researcher, and made sure they were lined up just the way he wanted them to be. He never left that space to eat his lunch and when it was time for us to go, he was heartbroken. It set off a lightbulb in my mind about how to cater to his interests. "I have to buy him more cars," I thought.

In addition to purchasing a slew of Hot Wheels and Matchbox-style cars, I began to observe some of his behaviors when it came to cars and vehicles. Whenever he got a new one, he would study it intently. He would sit it down on surfaces, move it back and forth, and look deeply at all of the details. However, this was not just his behavior with toy vehicles. One day we went to the store and a car was broken down in the parking lot. The hood was open and a man was working on it, and my son insisted I take him to see it. I was in awe—as a baby he was truly intrigued by cars and their inner workings. Knowing this, I exposed him to different car videos on YouTube and the internet, which even further piqued his interest. It was through YouTube videos that he discovered the illustrious world of monster trucks. Every video he watched, every game he played, and every song he listened to was about monster trucks. I had to graduate from the blissfully-priced ninety-nine-cent Hot Wheels and Matchbox cars to the bigger, badder, and more expensive monster trucks. He was obsessed with monster trucks, but he was also obsessed with learning. Unlike when his older brother was a toddler (nine years earlier), there was a multitude of videos, games, and songs on YouTube about monster trucks. YouTube was in its infancy around the time my oldest son was his age. He was obsessed with airplanes, but there were much fewer airplane videos on demand at that time, so he didn't get the same level of media exposure and learning in that way.

Similar to my daughter identifying letters on the back porch welcome mat, my youngest son also started demonstrating his knowledge of basic concepts I knew I had not taught him. By the time he was two, he already knew his letters, numbers, colors, and shapes mainly from watching videos, listening to songs, and playing online games related to cars and monster trucks. It occurred to me that perhaps if we presented knowledge to kids based on their interests, they would actually learn the material we are trying to teach them, without much effort on behalf of parents and teachers who work with them.

Not long after witnessing this, I was introduced to the concept of individualized learning and it gave me a thought. What if kids learned academic content through their own personal interests? When most kids are young, they gravitate toward some type of toy or cartoon or game. For me, it was Barbie dolls, my brother enjoyed Hot Wheels like my youngest son, and my oldest son was obsessed with airplanes and outer space. If young children are like sponges, then why not infuse what they're learning into dinosaurs or princesses or some character on YouTube or TV or whatever things they enjoy? They will still maintain their youthful innocence through play and exploration, but we can "sneak" in learning that will last them a lifetime. Within healthy limits, let them watch TV and use their iPads while they learn as much as they possibly can in the process.

Although children had limitations on play dates, "going places," and "doing things," kids who had resources were able to enjoy access to a wide range of freedoms within the confines of their homes during the quarantining/sheltering-in-place phase of the pandemic. On the other hand, there was a population of kids who saw the worst of the pandemic—parents who lost their jobs, some family members lost their lives, and they almost lost their minds because the walls were closing in on them both figuratively and literally. For some students, school provides a sense of normalcy, a place of refuge from undesirable environments, and caring adults who help guide them through difficulties and circumstances in ways their own parents and/or guardians are unable to. Whatever a child's circumstances were during that time, I can bet that no child was looking forward to going back to "normal." By "normal," I mean the traditional ways of school: the stand in a straight line, be quiet, sit still, don't talk to your friends, don't move around in class, model of institutionalization they have been subjected to. What did kids miss most about school? Their friends or the opportunity to make new ones and navigate the social landscape schools so conveniently provide. Unfortunately, when schools opened back up, schools were so worried about academic learning loss, they neglected to restore social and emotional learning properly and classrooms are still suffering as a result.

For the most part, the pandemic allowed kids to experience levels of freedom schools had not previously afforded them. They were free to go to the bathroom when they wanted to, free to wear what they wanted to, free to socialize via social media, text messages, or phones, and free to just *be*. And, as soon as the opportunity presented itself, we took those freely moving butterflies and shoved them back into cocoons as though they were still caterpillars. In the words of Lee Corso on ESPN's College Game Day, "Not so fast, my friend!" Did we really think that going back to business as usual was going to help young people suddenly become engrossed in their academic work and make up for all the lost learning they missed during quarantine? Was that a fair expectation? I think not.

A friend of mine, Nicolai Pizarro, who is a homeschool mom of two, author of two books, and social media influencer wrote a piece on June 22, 2020, after a presidential campaign rally was upended and sabotaged by a group of youth. This social media post adequately captures the idea that so many schools have it all wrong and that our children deserve better.

> If we are honest, many of us are NOT asking a generation of children that can sabotage a presidential rally via social media to return to an antiquated education model that does NOT work—in masks—so they can learn. We know that they can learn at home. THEY know that they can learn at home.
>
> We are asking them to return to school because 1. we don't trust ourselves 2. we don't want to 3. we don't trust them, 4. and/or we need for them to go somewhere while we work—the work we got after years of school which now doesn't let us take care of our kids but rather forces us to subject them to dysfunctional systems that don't work because we have to work! Phew!
>
> Our children SEE that guys.
>
> You don't think they do?

These children just sabotaged the president of the United States' rally.

These children are protesting in the streets.

These children have been raised thinking about monetizing content while we are still not.

I'm not judging us for having to go back to work and needing a place to hold our children for us. I get it. This capitalist structure sucks like that.

I am however questioning why so many of us are in denial? Do we really think our children have not connected the dots? Do we wonder why they don't trust themselves? Or why they don't trust US?

Do we ever stop to think that maybe they don't want to value or be motivated to trust, pay attention, and be engaged in school because they KNOW we are living through a real case of "the emperor's new clothes"?

I'm wondering why we don't see the disconnect that perhaps our children aren't engaged in school because school is what got us here and they—they don't want to be us!

If we want our children to listen to our guidance, we have to start by being honest with them.

If we must keep them in school because we have to work, we must also find a way to connect with them, advocate for them, engage them, and by all means NOT measure their worth and OUR connection to them by a school's curriculum or metrics.

And if we don't have to subject them to metal detectors and directed learning and tests and microaggressions and antiquated curriculums, then in defense of childhood and our future, we ought not to.

—June 22, 2020, Nicolai Pizzaro
Author of *Raising Readers* and *Ring the Alarm*

Once we settled back into the "new normal" of our schools, jobs, and public events, the social and emotional needs of our children should have been addressed first and foremost, with filling in the learning gaps a secondary priority. These babies have been through a lot, they have seen a lot, they have heard a lot, and though they are resilient and showed courage and strength during that time, they are still babies—our babies—and we needed to nurture their hearts and thoughts adequately before trying to shove a bunch of academic subject knowledge in their brains. They looked forward to being able to stand less than six feet away from their friends and teachers and give hugs. They wanted to share their feelings about sheltering in place, quarantining, the discomfort of wearing masks, constantly cleaning and sanitizing, the fear of the virus spread, and operating in the weird space that was defined by the global coronavirus pandemic of 2020.

Students are in need of the opportunity to learn subject material that will benefit them beyond graduation, but they also need the chance to feel comfortable, safe, and without fear in their educational environments. However, it seems now that we have overcome the restrictions Covid-19 put in place, they are less comfortable and more fearful in skool environments than they have ever been. Students are more intelligent and intuitive than we give them credit for and should be given autonomy in their educational journey—however, with this autonomy must come support and the ability for kids to be able to handle the responsibility and independence that come along with it. Certainly, there are basics all children need to master prior to allowing them complete freedom over what and how they learn. We should do a better job of ensuring mastery instead of rushing kids through a curriculum just to say they can do algebra in the sixth grade. Ultimately kids should be given a chance to explore their interests and get a taste of a variety of disciplines—*before* they spend hundreds of thousands of dollars on a college education just to have them drop out to go "find themselves."

The pandemic exposed so much of what students are missing from traditional environments and gave parents a much more wide-open view of who their children are and what they really need from their educational experiences. Since schools were reopened, many parents have realized that those needs are still not being met. The "return to normalcy" has been no match for the Covid slide that has been experienced by so many students. In addition to their academic deficiencies, some students have also been deprived of valuable experiences that contribute to their holistic well-being. Teacher turnover is at an all-time high and teacher morale has hit rock bottom, which leads to less-than-ideal classroom environments and circumstances, and students are left lost, confused, and unmotivated. In addition, the pandemic further stripped schools of the many classes and activities, such as art and music programs, that help encourage, inspire, and create balance for the strictly academic content they gain from their core courses. Again, students have been placed on the back burner of skoolz and skool districts, and parents are charged with filling in the many gaps that have opened up for students.

Students deserve better, but unless change happens quickly, their futures—our future—is in danger. It is time for skoolz and skool districts to establish and implement structures and resources that will help students achieve their potential and get them to the next level of greatness in their lives.

One of the interpretations of the word "education" originates from the word *educere*, which is derived from the French word *éduquer*, which means to "bring out" or "lead forth." So, if education is done right, we should seek to bring out the best in children and lead them forth into their own greatness. When my husband was a child, his favorite question was always "why?" He would ask why until he whittled down to the solutions that satisfied his curiosities. His mother, a wonderfully patient mother of eight, would humor him until he was satisfied. She never grew impatient or angry with him, but instead knew that by answering his questions, he would develop a greater understanding of the world around him and himself, and as a result, cultivated in him a sense of curiosity and a desire to become a lifelong learner. When children ask "why?" we should never shut them down or make them feel bad for asking, but instead provide answers that encourage them to continue to want to learn more and become problem solvers in the process. Students often ask insightful questions that could lead us all to the solutions to the many issues we face, but on too many occasions, we don't provide them the space to feel comfortable asking questions nor the tools to help them explore further. This should not be so. Let's not only allow children to ask "why," but seek to learn the "why" that exists inside of them.

In all of the understanding that children often seek to gain from us, how often do we take the time to try to understand them in return? Who are they? Why do they behave in the ways they do? What have they been exposed to? Exposure makes a huge difference in understanding the other two questions (who they are and why they behave the way they do). In trying to cook Brussels sprouts, I realized we don't often take the time to peel back the rotten layers that have been negatively exposed to get to the "good part." In our house, we try our best to eat vegetables with all of our meals and we had a bag of Brussels sprouts that was going bad. There were black specks of developing mold on the outer layers of leaves and around the bases. I cut off the blackened stems and began to peel away the leaves until I reached fresh leaves that were completely green. It took time and I ended up getting rid of almost half of the bag, but they were roasted to perfection, tender, and delicious. As much as my kids normally dislike Brussels sprouts, they ate them with no hesitation and even claimed they tasted good. I am in no way promoting cannibalism or suggesting we think of children like food, but the metaphor is clear: sometimes we have to peel back the layers of negative exposure that has occurred in a child's life to get to the best parts of who they are. It is often time-consuming, and it may even feel like your energy and efforts are wasted away, but the results are life-changing for the child and everyone around them.

DISSECTING THE "WHY?"

Regardless of the original reason why schools were created, we have to know by now that the students, our babies, must be at the core of every decision made, every dollar spent, and every minute we dedicate to their educational experience. Without them at the forefront, we make poor decisions that negatively impact their futures, funds are misallocated, and students are misguided into future plans that don't serve their purpose. Here are a couple of examples.

POOR DECISION-MAKING

The pandemic did an exceptional job of exposing exactly what happens when poor decisions or no decisions are made, and one such example is in how skoolz handled the opening of their doors after the summer of sheltering in place. So many skoolz were wishy-washy and couldn't make up their minds about how they wanted to approach the return to school. Some wanted to remain completely remote, some wanted hybrid options, and some wanted to pretend like there was no health threat and send everybody to school with no safety and health measures in place. Those skoolz that remained completely or primarily remote had children who suffered a great deal of learning loss. The skoolz that were hybrid created additional stress for families and children who couldn't keep up with the fluctuating schedule. Skoolz that opened with no concrete safety measures ended up having mass outbreaks of cases that caused educational and emotional disruptions and burdened the health of students and their families.

However, there were some schools that chose to open their doors, but established very strict and effective health and safety guidelines that not only allowed their students to thrive academically, but also kept their campuses safe and healthy as a whole. These were schools that chose not to politicize the decisions they made for their students, but instead operated with common sense guidelines based on factual research. The students in these schools were able to thrive both during and after the pandemic and have benefited from the excellence in decision-making that their schools made on their behalf.

MISALLOCATED FUNDS

I remember being in an integrated math-science technology magnet program in high school. The first of its kind in my hometown, I recall the renovations they did to my school and how they added a bunch of fancy furniture to the classrooms. But even with all of that in place, there was a lonely frog, shrink-wrapped in plastic packaging that got me the most excited. My sophomore year, I took biology and as an aspiring neurosurgeon, I felt a great connection to this frog and couldn't wait to cut him up to see what his insides were like. It would be my first experience as a "surgeon" and I vowed to be careful with him and learn all I could in the dissection lab. But it never happened. I walked around my biology classroom all school year long, with the frog by my side, unopened, and uncut. How much did it really cost to purchase a class set of dissectible frogs for us to have that experience? While I remember the fancy building that they invested the money into, it was eventually torn down for an upgraded facility and I'm still left with the sting of *not* dissecting the frog.

What really matters to the students? Not just what matters now, but what will matter five, ten, fifteen years from now when school is no longer there for them? What impact will have been made in their lives to motivate them, propel them to their next achievements, or help them have better lives overall? Is it the ABCs and 123s or is it something more? What will we say and do that will really make a difference to them beyond the classroom and beyond the walls of school environments? I told the story about the frog not because the frog mattered, but because the experience I wanted to have by dissecting the frog is something that could have changed my trajectory, especially as an aspiring surgeon. The stuff never matters. It's always the lessons, memories, and insights the stuff creates that matter.

We invest in what we value, so the question is, what do we value most? Do we care more about what it looks like (buildings, fancy extras) than we should? So many times, the adults (parents, teachers, and administrators) place value and make decisions on time and resources that the students don't always get the most benefit from. When in budget meetings and during curriculum planning sessions, the value for the student should always be at the forefront rather than making things just "look good." School districts and systems love to talk about state-of-the-art facilities and innovative curricula, but how are the students actually benefiting from these "talking points"? Is the infrastructure in place to implement these elements or are the decisions to purchase and/or invest based on a "hope" things will work out? Our babies have been through a lot since 2020 and we owe them our very best—our very best provision in school buildings, our very best teaching and nurturing efforts as teachers, and our very best love as parents. They are the reason why we do what we do, so let's put them at the forefront of it all and give them the power to lead the way.

One of the most powerful stories I heard about a student was told by the late Sir Ken Robinson at a conference I attended. He told the story of a young man who was asked by his high school teacher what he wanted to be when he graduated from high school. While others in his class told of their dreams to become doctors, lawyers, and financial advisors, this particular student proudly declared that he wanted to become a firefighter. His teacher was surprised and disappointed by his response and told him, "Son, that's a 'child's dream' and it's time for you to grow up. You are way too smart to want to become a firefighter." But that student knew the power in his purpose and chose not to listen to his teacher. He decided to pursue his "child's dream" as an adult and became a firefighter despite his teacher's lack of support. Many years passed by and the teacher and his wife got into a horrifying car accident that could have claimed both of their lives, if it had not been for the student who was "too smart" to become a firefighter. He saved them on that fateful day, but what if he had actually taken what the teacher said to heart? What if he said, "Maybe he's right. I'll go to college and become a financial advisor." Maybe, he would have saved them from mounting debt, but he wouldn't have been able to save their lives.

A similar situation occurred when I was working with students to help them navigate their college and career pathways. A young lady came to me and said that she wanted to do hair when she graduated from high school, but so many people had been telling her that she was "too smart" to become a hairstylist. Are you kidding me? Hairstylists are some of the most creative and intelligent people I know. I really wish the "oh-so-intelligent grown folks" would stop telling young people they are "too smart" to be doing what they love and want to do. In my own life, one of my favorite jobs was being a recruiter for an online master's and doctorate program. In this position, I traveled to K–12 schools to recruit teachers by providing information about postgraduate options that didn't require traveling every month or weekend to do so. I was in my hometown at one of the middle schools and ran into a teacher who was full-time, but who had been a substitute teacher when I was a K–12 student. She asked me how I was doing and I told her I was great, but her response was unexpected and unwelcomed. "I'm disappointed in you," was her response. I was confused and taken aback.

"What do you mean?" I replied.

"I thought you were going to be a doctor or a lawyer or something like that." My confusion turned into offense and disgust and I thought: *WOW! How sad it is that we have been programmed to think the only way you can be successful is by spending all your time, money, and brain cells to obtain degrees for the sake of holding a title?* In the grand scheme of things, these titles mean nothing and have no bearing on a person's happiness and well-being, especially if they are not operating in their purpose and passion. Yes, perhaps I *could* have been a doctor or lawyer, but I ultimately chose another path and there is no way I should have been berated for doing so.

All things are not for everybody and there is a saying that "If you do what you love, you will never work a day in your life." So, if you go through all the trouble to get a bunch of fancy degrees and all these certifications to hold a title, but yet, you're miserable, are you really smart? Sounds pretty dumb to me. Smart people choose to open cleaning businesses or decide to create and become artists because it's what they love and want to do. As a result, they are operating in their purpose and satisfied with their lives, which should be the measure of success—not degrees, status, or titles. I know people who have left prestigious law practices because the eighty-hour workweek wasn't worth losing their family and personal time or their health over. Just because you are "smart" by school standards, doesn't make you "smart" if you choose to continue your education and are not happy with the life you have once you have reached that outcome.

People who are happy doing what they do are the smartest people out there because they choose themselves over other people's ideas of what they should be. By doing so, they give their all and they truly make a difference in the lives of the people they touch. When you think about the people who have truly made an impact in the lives of others, do you even know where they went to school and got their degrees from? Probably not. Of course, there is Dr. Martin Luther King Jr. associated with Morehouse College or Phil Knight with the University of Oregon, but those are exceptions. There are so many other impactful people out in the world, but they are very rarely identified by their schools unless their impact is based on what they did while they were in school (star athletes and their corresponding sports teams usually fit into this category). If we let students just be and do and cultivate their inner talents, passions, and abilities instead of forcing them into school-imposed boxes, we will build a nation of people who are happy, healthy, and will in essence be better for everyone. But it starts with the students. It begins with cultivating the youngest, most impressionable minds and hearts, by taking the time to nurture them, but most importantly to *listen* to them. Let's not allow our old minds that have been tainted by the realities and tragedies of our own lives to squeeze out the imaginations, high hopes, and vivid dreams of the babies. We need their creativity. We need their far-fetched ideas and thoughts. We need their belief in themselves and in the world so that we can have world peace and feed every hungry person. It's the fuel of a bright future and we don't need it to be extinguished by the limitations of skoolz—we need it to be brought forth by people. Only *we* the *people* can give these students what they need to change the world.

CHAPTER 9
WE R . . .

The collective, the village, and the ones we can count on to make the world of education better than the way we found it. There was a powerful song released in 1985 that talked about lending a helping hand and making a better day for others. The lyrics of this song, which were at the core of the USA for Africa movement, not only rang true for eradicating hunger in the 1980s, but are also relevant for saving education in the times we are living in now.

This is our work *together*, so why are so many of us working against each other? There is no way we can hope to achieve a collective goal of student success if we can't come together in the best interest of students. I have seen far too many instances in which one teacher dislikes another teacher, or an administrator "can't stand" a parent, or some other issue where the adults can't get it together and the kids suffer. I know some circumstances are difficult—I get it. But we have to overcome those challenges by finding solutions that allow us to set our differences aside and put students first.

It is my hope this book has inspired you (in whatever capacity you are in at this time) to do something to improve skoolz and skool systems. There are so many ideas for how and why education could be changed for the better, but there is no one silver bullet to fix all of the many problems that exist. I've heard many suggestions for how to best create meaningful change—from putting more money into special education to holding parents more accountable for their children's behavior to individualizing the learning environment for students. The proposed ways of "fixing" our skool systems seem endless. However, the first step we must take in implementing real change is to understand that *we* the people possess the power to change. It is unfortunate, but for far too long, the people who make up the systems have felt powerless and as though they cannot have an impact or make a difference. On the contrary, students, parents, teachers, and administrators are the most powerful people in the educational system, and we can't let the systems be the dictator for how we (and the people we care about) experience education. Regardless of your background or role, the power you have in making a difference in the educational landscape is significant . . . you just have to know how to use it. This chapter is a "Power Playbook" guide featuring ideas on how to do so.

PART 1: POWER PLAYBOOK FOUNDATIONAL TOOLS FOR SUCCESS

This section is for *everyone*. These tools are beneficial for any person in any situation and can serve as a light as we all work together to make schools better for the children being served.

TOOL 1: KINDNESS AND AN OPEN MIND

Times are hard and there is no reason why anyone should make things any harder by being rude, cold, or callous to another person. Times are hard for everyone, and it is important for all of us to show one another some grace. In one of my previous chapters, I mentioned how much easier it is to attract bees with honey rather than vinegar and this holds true for almost any interaction you may have with other people. I'm not saying you should be a "pushover," but there is a special power in "killing people with kindness." Dealing with schools, especially if you have a specific issue or personal situation you want to change or address, can be incredibly difficult and frustrating and it's not always easy to keep your cool when interacting with others. However, it is much easier to accomplish your goals if you find ways to approach people with kindness leading the way. As upset as you may be, leading a conversation with a positive energy will (more often than not) get the outcomes you want much faster and more efficiently than cursing people out and getting an attitude.

I recall having a "conversation" about charter schools with a person who was on the school board of a local school district, and she almost bit my head off when I started discussing some of the benefits of charter schools. My stance on schools is this: Whatever works best for your child is what's best, regardless of the type of school or learning environment they are in and it is up to families to decide that for their children. However, when I brought it up, she got loud, indignant, and incredibly confrontational. Her reactions were verbally violent to the point where I thought she wanted to attack me physically and she completely closed herself to hearing my point of view. It was disappointing because that interaction gave me the impression that she didn't have all families' best interests at heart and was only looking at educational choice from a bottom-line point of view. As a person elected by her community to be responsible for helping make decisions about children's education, I fully expected her to support the traditional public school system she worked for. However, instead of taking time to hear me out to gain insights to improve *all* school environments, she attacked me. As a result, the door was closed on a potentially enlightening interaction for both of us and hostility won out over kindness. Her negative energy shut down what could have been a very thought-provoking discussion that could have led to positive change. Although this interaction occurred many years ago, it is still very fresh in my mind and that moment caused me to look at her differently.

There are a lot of variables floating around in the world of education and our babies' futures are at stake, but the best way to approach this very delicate topic is to "be kind and keep an open mind." The world is changing much faster than education systems are, and close-mindedness and the inability to kindly connect with others contribute to why. Becoming kinder with others would be a great way to advance progress in this field (and to be quite honest, in other areas such as politics and business as well).

TOOL 2: KNOWLEDGE OF LAWS, POLICIES, AND RIGHTS

There is a biblical verse that states, "My people perish for lack of knowledge," and this statement is unfortunately true for many children in schools. They are perishing academically because of a lack of knowledge in the system policies, rights, and laws that either benefit them or create challenges. For example, many parents are unaware that public schools are required, by law, to meet the educational needs of students who qualify for special education services. Some parents are also not aware that there is always a "space" for their child in the school they are assigned to in places where students are assigned based on where they live. With the many differences that exist in laws and policies from district to district and state to state, it can be difficult to keep up with all of the liberties and barriers that can factor into educating children. For teachers and administrators, it can be equally frustrating. As a teacher, I faced the hardship of dealing with changes to the certification requirements at the same time I was working to achieve them. I also went through the trouble of applying for, getting accepted to, and completing the first year of a doctorate program only to learn I wouldn't be able to receive additional pay due to changes in the state requirements.

As you navigate the process of advocating for change in education, it is important to keep your eyes on the prize and learn the political influences on policies and structure. I have learned that some educational ideals are aligned with certain political parties. Regardless of your party affiliation or the political landscape of your state, it is important to know how political nuances can impact the work being done to achieve the changes you want to see.

TOOL 3: KNOWING WHICH BATTLES TO PICK

Very similar to knowing the laws, policies, and regulations surrounding educational landscapes, it is equally important to know who and what is worth going after. Some organizations and policies are behemoths that require a great deal of money and large numbers of people to challenge, where others may be changed with a few letters and/or phone calls. I'm not saying some of these bigger battles are not worth fighting, but please be sure to calculate the costs before taking them on. Ask yourself: Do I have the resources? Do I have the time? Do I have the social and/or emotional capacity? Although we are often frustrated about the flaws, inconsistencies, and failures of schools and school districts on a broad scale, it's important to consider what changes can be made within our small microcosms that could potentially have a ripple effect on the bigger picture.

We all have the power to make a difference in our respective schools and school systems, but it has to be strategic and sometimes it's better to focus on winning a series of small battles that leads to winning the war. Eating the elephant one bite at a time over a period of time is much easier than trying to choke down the whole animal. Even with that in mind, there is another very important question you have to ask yourself in order to decide how to approach rallying for change and improvement in the educational arena:

Ultimately, if I take this on and win, how long will it take for the impact to be made and will it still matter by that time? This question leads me to Tool number 4.

TOOL 4: KNOWING YOUR LIMITATIONS AND UNDERSTANDING TIMELINES FOR CHANGE AND IMPLEMENTATION

Policies often take a long time to change and even when they do, it may take even longer for those changes to take effect. So what happens in the meantime? It is possible to fight for a policy or a change in regulation impacting elementary school children that may not take effect until those children reach middle or high school. There has to be something that will provide relief and a solution for those undesired circumstances while you wait. In addition to your ultimate goal, what are some things that can be done immediately to make your situation better?

Perhaps you are fighting to change teacher certification guidelines and in the middle of your efforts, you move to another state or take a job outside of the classroom. Will it still matter to you? Will you still have the passion for change once you move away from the area or step away from the position or profession? Certainly, it can be impactful for those that come after you, but will you have the same motivation and energy to continue to push for change? If not, have you been surrounded by others who will continue the fight? There has to be a support system for your efforts, or they could all come tumbling down if you are no longer connected to them.

PART II: POWER PLAYBOOK SOLUTIONS FOR ADMINISTRATORS, TEACHERS, PARENTS, AND STUDENTS

This section provides ideas for solutions based on roles within schools and school systems. It doesn't contain any earth-shattering breaking news—just some gentle reminders of things that we can do within our respective positions to make the greatest impact on those we have influence over.

ADMINISTRATORS

CARE about teachers in the same way you care about students. If a student isn't feeling well, running a fever, or is having issues at home, we have empathy for them and even encourage them to go home and feel better before returning to school. Why is this sometimes not the case for teachers? In order for teachers to perform their best, they should be given the opportunity to take mental health days, recharge their batteries, and just feel better before returning back to the classroom. Most teachers truly care about their students and don't want to be out for the sake of being out, but sometimes just need a break. Or perhaps, they already have the tough job of taking care of others (young children, aging parents, special needs family members, etc.) and need to feel supported if they have to step away from the classroom to do so. For teachers, having work-life balance and the reassurance of administrative support to care for the people they love the most often translates into them giving 100 percent of their professional selves. I know that substitute teachers can be hard to come by and classrooms are already overcrowded. However, providing a strong sense of balance can go a long way to reduce teacher absenteeism and could ultimately help prevent teacher turnover rates.

GIVE teachers adequate time to get to know their students before requiring that they dive into academic content. In my opinion, one of the biggest mistakes that skool systems and administrators make at the start of the school year is providing teachers with a timeline that requires them to jump headfirst into rules, curriculum, and lessons without making space at the start of school to allow teachers and students to get to know one another. I cannot think of a subject area topic that is so important it should be prioritized over building relationships with students. If the topic or subject area is that valuable, then the curriculum should be used and incorporated in a way that allows teachers to get to know students and vice versa. When students have the opportunity to establish trust with their teachers, it allows for teachers to establish an environment of mutual respect, which minimizes behavior issues and makes large, overcrowded classrooms easier to manage.

EMPOWER your teachers and trust their expertise. Teacher morale is at an all-time low. The turnover rate is astronomical, and we need teachers more than ever. Micromanaging capable individuals who have earned their right to be in the classroom is ineffective and demoralizing. If there is a teacher who needs more guidance, provide it in the best way you can, but build their confidence in the process and give them room to earn your trust. Take the time to get to know what your teachers need most and how you can best support them.

LISTEN to teacher suggestions and ideas, no matter how far-fetched they may seem. They are in the trenches every single day, doing everything in their power to help kids learn and maintain a safe environment. Sometimes their ideas may be a bit "out there," but it usually comes from a good place. Get to the core of what they are suggesting and try to find a common ground if you find their ideas to be too radical. I remember telling my principal I wanted my students to design my walls with graffiti art and that I would supply the spray paint. I knew it was a bit much to ask, but I was hoping that by suggesting it, we could come up with other ways to make the walls in the building more aesthetically appealing. If there is a will, there is a way. Unfortunately, the idea was shut down without further discussion. Even if he wasn't really going to entertain the idea, it would have been nice to feel like my thoughts about beautifying the place were valuable.

LISTEN and ACT when teachers tell you something about their students that could be detrimental in the future no matter how small it may seem initially. If a student has been harassing, threatening, or bullying a student, PLEASE LISTEN and ACT. Teachers spend more time with their students than anybody else and can often sense when a situation has the potential to escalate into something worse. It is absolutely heartbreaking and infuriating to hear stories about students who repeatedly cause harm to teachers or other students after these instances have been ignored by administrative staff members.

ALLOW teachers creative freedom and out of the box ways of reaching their students. I had a student that only wanted to play basketball and could never sit still in class. His constant movement all over the class was very disruptive, but he really couldn't help it. Sometimes he just wanted to lie on the floor to do his work, and sometimes I would allow him to do so. However, I was always worried that one of the administrators would come in and reprimand both him and me. One day, I coordinated the opportunity for him to spend some time in the gym with the PE teacher so he could learn more about ratios in math. He left my class and had to shoot hoops with the teacher and another student to see how many free throws, three-point shots, and layups were achieved by each person. When he came back to the class, he had a greater understanding of the concept of ratios, but there was no way I would be able to do that every day without worrying it would be an issue with the principal and assistant principal. Teachers shouldn't have to live in fear of being admonished when they want to try new things and implement out of the box methods of learning for their students. There should be opportunities for creative outlets that work well for everyone, and administrators should work to find ways to support these ideas.

MINIMIZE the workload as much as possible for teachers. Reduce the number of meetings that you have with your teaching staff. Planning periods are important for teachers to work on the many tasks that they are faced with daily, and no two days are exactly alike. Find ways to send pertinent information in an email, weekly staff newsletter, or utilize a software platform that will allow for collaboration and sharing of ideas in an asynchronous form so they don't have to be in more meetings and can use their planning periods for the many other responsibilities they're faced with daily. Investing in tools that will increase teacher effectiveness and save time is a win-win and certainly worth spending budgeting dollars on. Sometimes teachers need less professional development and more tools and resources to help them get more stuff done.

EXPLAIN the WHY to teachers *and* students! Especially in situations that require change, students and teachers want to know "why" and I think it is important for administrators to explain it to them! One of the most irritating things those in authority can do is to implement changes and create rules without a valid explanation. Please don't use your administrative power to withhold information and resources from your staff, students, and parents—give them a *real reason* for why you have chosen to make a decision. I understand you can't always give the details, but make it make sense! It helps people to be more accepting of change and get on board with your overall vision and ideas.

REMEMBER what it was like to be in teachers' shoes. Sometimes administrators lose sight of their origins when they have been in a position of power and have to see things from a different viewpoint. What are the things that frustrated you when you were a classroom teacher? How could you make a difference for the teachers you supervise that would have helped you when you were walking in their shoes? Don't allow schools and school systems make you callous and insensitive to the needs of your teachers, staff, and students. Bureaucracy, politics, and the status quo can be easy to accept and fall into when you are in a place of power. However, please do your best to utilize your power and position to make the difference you have always wanted to see.

TEACHERS

This book has barely scratched the surface of the myriads of challenges existing in many of our schools regarding teachers. I have read or heard about the extreme issues—teachers being attacked (or even shot) by students, teachers being forced to work all day without a break, and teachers being required to check classrooms after a bomb threat—and my heart goes out to those in these ridiculously unbelievable circumstances. Sadly, I believe teachers are those in the educational equation who feel the most powerless and the least motivated to make a change, but they are the most important component within schools. Could and would schools exist if teachers were not there? Administrators and district officials cannot hold enough space to make up for a void if teachers made a mass exodus from schools. Teachers often feel weak and incapacitated, especially when faced with difficult decisions or circumstances and they don't have legal, moral, or administrative support to back them up.

I remember the defeat I felt when I was going against the district-mandated curriculum to teach concepts my kids desperately needed. My administrators didn't support my efforts and I was often called out for not being on track with the curriculum and I always felt like I was having to hide and cover up my lessons when administrators came in to observe. I remember the disappointment I felt when I was forced out of the classroom halfway through my certification program because federal regulations didn't want teachers with provisional credentials to serve as full-time teachers—even though I had *already* been teaching for two years. I remember the despair I felt when I was working to teach five classes of students during a pandemic while also working to help my own four children through the challenges of distance learning and the uncertainty of a virus that was ravaging the world. Teachers are often faced with so many issues that lead to defeat, disappointment, and despair, but feel like there is nothing they can do about their situation.

There are many platforms that exist to serve as a sounding board for complaints, but we have to find ways to share ideas for making the job of teaching easier and to lift each other up. It is my goal that this section serves as ideas to help make your time in the classroom more manageable, and that if collectively practiced, could potentially snowball into big changes in the classroom and beyond. I do not know your specific classroom circumstances, but these are just some general ideas that can help you help students from a social, emotional, and academic perspective and hopefully make you feel more empowered in the classroom.

TAKE the time to build relationships with your students—and be *nice* (as much as possible). Whenever I ask kids about their favorite teacher and why that person was their favorite, they often say because they are "nice." Certainly, there are times when you have to "put your foot down" and show tough love, but kids know if you really do care about them, so express it. Sometimes a hug from a teacher or the words "I care about you" are the only time throughout their day that love is expressed to them, so be genuine and show it when you can. This is a process and it requires you to be vulnerable and open with your students. You cannot stoop to their levels when they are being petty or have a terrible attitude. Many of the behaviors seen in the classroom are an "acting out" of whatever they are experiencing personally or see in their homes/communities. You may or may not be able to reach them all, but that's okay. Connect with those who are open and have an open heart for all the others who may come around later. Some kids are guarded and don't allow themselves to get close to people, so you may never know (at least in the moment) if they know how much you care about them, but show them love and nurture anyway. Sometimes it's the ones that say the least that are most impacted by your care.

ALLOW your students to see you as a human. It is okay to admit you don't know something, or apologize when you are wrong. It is okay to cry sometimes—there are some instances that call for tears and children can respect you for being able to tap into your emotions. But whatever you do, don't cry when students make classroom management hard or overwhelming—it is like blood to a shark. Students will exploit your emotions and hold it over your head and you will never be able to establish and/or maintain a conducive learning environment. It's okay to make mistakes, apologize, and ask for forgiveness. Help students understand that even teachers are not perfect and there are things you can improve upon and do better.

Within the right environment and with the proper guidance, you may even solicit their feedback and suggestions for improvement. Learning how to lead a restorative circle is a great way to have open dialogue about topics that are sensitive or require additional guidance. There are excellent resources at https://www.werestoremore.com/ to help with these processes.

ESTABLISH a mutual respect with students from the very beginning and draw the line between teacher and student. You can be a cool teacher and role model without operating like you are their friend. Don't share your personal social media accounts with them and whatever you do, don't get into "playful" verbal confrontations with students. Some kids are incredibly savvy and will rip you to shreds if you trigger them. Leave children's verbal interactions to the children. I recall a situation in which a teacher's aide was playing the "dozens" with a student and he lost—got totally disrespected and his feelings were hurt. He then turned around and reported what the student said to the administration, which got the student in trouble. This is a total misuse of power and should not have happened without him also getting written up. Teachers should never provoke students to behave in negative ways and then use their power to have them disciplined without them also receiving a disciplinary consequence in return.

USE your teacher power. By nature, I tend to buck against systems I don't agree with or that I feel don't make sense. As a teacher, one of my greatest survival techniques was to "do what I do" in the classroom. For me, the required curriculum and prefabricated lesson plans served as a guideline to coincide with the academic needs of my students. Although it may have ruffled a few feathers, I did what I needed to do to help my students fill in gaps and achieve their goals. As a classroom teacher, you sometimes have to use your freedoms to do what's best for your students, and ultimately for you.

TALK the talk as you walk the walk—normalize high-level vocabulary, *especially* with younger children. Use the vocabulary of the subject you are focused on . . . especially with younger children. Tips and tools like Keep-Change-Flip are useful for helping children solve problems. However, if they don't know what multiplying by the reciprocal is, they will be clueless when it's presented to them on a test or in higher-level math classes. Why not start the process of helping kids understand the language of the subject from the very beginning? I recall training kindergarten teachers who were wondering how to better explain science concepts to their students. It never occurred to them that if they speak using science vocabulary and explain to their students what it meant, that it would actually stick. Just as my mother didn't talk baby talk with my brother and I, and I never talked "baby talk" with my own children, teachers should never "dumb down" complex vocabulary and concepts. I remember explaining the difference between a physical and a chemical reaction to my children when I was holding them in my arms and preparing meals for the family. When cracking an egg, I told them the egg had undergone a physical reaction. Though it would be difficult, the insides of the egg could be poured back into the shell and "Humpty Dumpty" could be repaired. However, when I dropped the insides of Humpty Dumpty into the hot frying pan, I explained that the egg was undergoing a chemical reaction because it could never go back to its original form. When I think of kindergartners, I think of the concept of potential and kinetic energy states. I told the teachers that when the children are moving about all over the classroom and they want them to calm down, they could start off the school year (while establishing classroom norms) by explaining the concept of potential and kinetic energy. That way, when they are overly active in the classroom, they could say something like: "Hey, kids, let's turn this kinetic energy into potential energy," and their students would understand.

I walked into a first-grade classroom one day and heard a first-grade teacher using the words addends and sums when breaking down an addition problem to a group of students that knew exactly what she was talking about. The students were getting a strong foundation of mathematical terminology and for them, it was nothing unusual. If we want children to have an understanding of higher-level concepts, why not teach them the vocabulary that coincides with the most basic forms of these concepts? This terminology is vital as they advance through higher levels of the subject matter they are learning.

PARENTS

One of the greatest gifts you can give to a teacher is an attitude of gratitude, partnership, and support. I am not telling you the teacher is always right all the time, but for many children (especially those in elementary school), the teacher spends as much if not more time than parents do, so they are able to see behaviors and have a different understanding of your child than you do. I remember having a student who displayed incredibly strange behaviors at school. However, whenever she was in the presence of her parents, she was a completely different person and never carried out those weird mannerisms. There are some kids who act the exact same way at home as they do at school, and others that contradict their home behaviors with what they do at school for a variety of reasons. Sometimes parents take offense when they are being informed by teachers that their children are behaving "out of character" from their perspective. With this in mind, it is important to gain a full understanding of all the circumstances if situations occur at school that contradict what you know of your child's character.

HAVE GRACE FOR TEACHERS

After the time parents spent with their children during the pandemic, nobody should have more grace and understanding for teachers than parents. Imagine having to come up with lesson plans, manage behavior, and implement lessons (while also providing evaluative feedback to students, attending meetings, and responding to parents) for not just one or two children, but for a whole classroom of twenty, twenty-five, and sometimes more than thirty students. It is a lot to handle and as much as teachers want to meet the needs of each child individually, it is almost impossible to do so in many circumstances. I know that sometimes we as parents get frustrated with teachers and administrators' slow response time in communication or their inability to give their undivided attention to their students and families, but unfortunately, most of them are just not able to do so. The best thing a parent can do is to work with them from a place of compassion for their daily demands. When working with them on a personal situation, try to understand their perspective and hear them out prior to criticizing or going off on them. And when you do, try your best to do it from a place of kindness—it always helps the situation, especially for the child. If they are young, it is sometimes difficult for them to distinguish between your anger for a situation and your anger for a person. If they sense you have issues with a particular teacher or administrator, it may cause them to act out without understanding why.

CHOOSE THE RIGHT SCHOOL ENVIRONMENT FOR YOUR CHILD AND YOUR FAMILY'S CIRCUMSTANCES

Sometimes, no matter how closely you partner with teachers and administrators in a school, it just isn't the right fit for your child, and you have to find a place that would serve them best.

I recall a time in which we would receive phone calls regarding our son's behaviors at school, which included small, nit-picky things that could have easily been corrected with redirection. At the time, he was going to a school that was closely guarded by gatekeepers that required at least twenty-four hours of notice prior to a parent coming to a classroom. However, one day my husband was going to a father-daughter dance at the school and had the opportunity to see firsthand what was happening in the classroom. The behaviors the teachers claimed were such a "menace" in the classroom was no different than what other children, in the same class, were doing and the other kids were not being reprimanded for it. This helped us see he was being wrongfully targeted and treated poorly by his teachers. Of course, we brought this up to the administration and the teacher in question, and although the complaints against him decreased, we knew it was not the best environment for him and changed his school the next year.

No school is perfect and we don't always have the luxury of selecting our child's school, but if you do have the resources and wherewithal to do so, please do your research. So many people purchase homes in neighborhoods because they have looked at test scores and what looks good on paper without doing a deep dive to determine if the skool district in which they are investing would be right for their child. Find Facebook groups and other social media outlets that will provide real feedback regarding the schools you are looking into. Ask other parents whose kids go to school there and find out what they value. Just because a parent says a school is good for *their* child doesn't mean the same school is good for *your* child. Make sure all of the pieces add up to ensure a school is worth your child going there. If you live in a place that sends kids to schools based on a geographical zone or district, please be sure to get some insights into schools that are close by to find out if the neighboring schools are just as good. It is an unfortunate situation to purchase a home to be in a certain school district that gets "redistricted." So many families get caught up in the idea that they are purchasing a home in a "good school district," but are left out of being able to send their kids to the schools they bought the home for because the county or district has shifted the lines based on population, resources, or political interests.

Prior to attending the school where he would complete his secondary education, my son was what I would call "educationally oppressed." He struggled through so many schools because they didn't have the capacity for his high energy and next-level intelligence. He is a deep, philosophical thinker, but is a child who couldn't sit still in the classroom because the way information was presented didn't stimulate his way of processing the information. For years, he felt like he wasn't smart because his grades were not high and he rarely got praise from his teachers. In addition to many schools just not being the right fit, we moved several times so he attended nine different skoolz in nine years. He ended up in a place that allows him to be a free thinker and he excelled academically. I spent many years in despair trying to figure out how to best help him and many of his struggles within schools helped serve as inspiration for this book. It took a long time, but he graduated from a place that nurtures his intelligence.

In the event that your child's skool is not the most ideal fit for your child(ren) and you don't have much other educational choice, you have to know what it takes to help cultivate that environment in a way that can help your child thrive. This is where the powers of persuasion, presence, and participation come into play. You have to have an understanding of the type of school your children attend and how to leverage the powers that drive them to best meet the needs of your child(ren). Get to know administrators, members of the school board or board of directors, and other school influencers to learn the ins and outs of your child's skool environment and what you need to do to help them navigate in order to have the best experience possible.

READ THE LABELS AND NOURISH YOUR CHILD'S BRAIN

Feed your children nutrient-dense foods that will help them focus and concentrate, especially in the morning. Certain foods, such as Flaming Hot Cheetos, Fruit by the Foot, and Gushers are *filled* with harmful ingredients that not only destroy young bodies, but also alters the way children process information and their ability to pay attention and learn. Many breakfast cereals also contain these harmful ingredients and while breakfast is the most important meal of the day, loading kids' bodies and brains with sugar and harmful preservatives to start their day is disadvantageous. This is not a "health nut" declaration because I know that healthy foods are not always affordable or easy to come by, but there are alternatives to the high-sugar, preservative-laden foods that make their way into our babies' bodies and alter their moods and behaviors. Mental health and acumen are very closely related to what we eat, so we must refrain from feeding children a diet that will cause them to act out in school, or (even worse) jeopardize their long-term mental and physical well-being. There are many ingredients found in foods that can cause adverse reactions, including monosodium glutamate (MSG), red 40, and high fructose corn syrup. In addition, there are many studies that specifically outline how these and their ingredients wreak havoc on the human body and brain. However, it is important for you to do your own research to decide what foods to eliminate or add and make the best decisions for your family's nutritional and financial needs.

STUDENTS

If you are mature enough to read this book, you are mature enough to be able to research and speak up for yourself. Adults don't have all the answers and sometimes a student's voice is incredibly powerful. However, it all depends on how you use it. When properly put to use, a student's voice can have a major impact on the educational landscape. However, when students are unable to effectively articulate their needs, not only does it fall on deaf ears, but it can also give the perception that you are rebellious and resistant to the learning process. As you might have guessed, rebellion in my opinion is not always a bad thing, but as my experiences have shown, rebellion can limit your opportunities and access. With that in mind, let me help you get what you need and want without having to go through the headaches and heartaches I endured when I voiced my thoughts, beliefs, and opinions.

Learn how to best communicate with teachers, coaches, and administrators. Find out how they best receive communication. If they prefer email, email them, if they want you to set up time to meet with them after/before school or during their office hours, take advantage of those times. Once you have secured their attention, whether in writing or verbally, find a way to ask questions without coming across as disrespectful, which can be difficult. There were so many times I have approached coaches in particular with a tone they found to be offensive, when that was not my intent at all. If you are upset about something, it is best to wait until you have calmed down and taken the time to organize your thoughts and ideas. Have a friend, parent, or other trusted advisor talk with you through the conversation you plan to have or to read over the email you plan to send. Communication is key and ensuring you approach those in power in a way it will be well-received is one of the best ways to accomplish what you are looking to do.

Whatever your goals and plans are, please *don't allow schools to define your intelligence, talents, and abilities.* You are greater than your grades and are smarter than the systems. For those of you who have always excelled in school, take time to discover the many ways your academic prowess can be translated into real-world experiences and can be used for more than getting high test scores. No matter what others may say—follow your dreams and listen to your heart. Sometimes we have a burning passion and love for something that exists deep within us that others don't know about and can't understand. Find ways to cultivate it! Find trusted advocates that can mentor you in your chosen areas of interest. Sometimes these people will be teachers and coaches you know from school, but they don't have to be. Reach out to community leaders, social media influencers and others that have traveled the path you aspire to take in order to find mentors and adult advisors who can help guide you on your journey.

SO WHAT'S NEXT? (CALL TO ACTION)

What will *you* do with what you have? Are you going to give the power to skoolz, skool districts, and systems to control your destiny? Are you going to lean into their policies, curricula, and grading guidelines to dictate your worth and all you can gain out of life? Are you going to allow the limitations of your role within these systems to determine the power you have to make a difference? Or are you going to stand firm in who you are and who you've been called to be to chart your own path and make the way yours even if the proverbial "theys" create barriers to your destiny?

For some of us, the journey is tough and difficult, and we may have to get a little more creative, a little bolder, a little more rebellious to get to where we want and need to be. One of the greatest pieces of wisdom my father has ever shared with me is that "nothing worth having ever comes easy." We know that to get to where we want to be is not easy, but it's worth it. So, let's do this. Let's not give *our* power and intelligence to the skoolz and systems that are designed to ultimately strip us of our control and influence . . .

Skoolz R dumb. Skoolz R powerless. *We* the people R smart. *We* the people R powerful. *We* the people R the solution we have been looking for and *now* is the time for us to bring those solutions to life . . .

I have written some things within these pages that may upset you or that you just don't believe are true or that do not resonate with your personal experiences. You may choose to criticize my blunt, straightforward style, not-so-perfect grammar (it has been a long time since I taught language arts, gimme a break!), or anecdotal accounts of events that may seem far-fetched or outrageous. Conversely, this book may have you saying "Amen/Ameen" or closing the pages to clap your hands in agreement. Or, you may read it and think to yourself *Meh, whatever*. Regardless of what you think of my writing style or how you feel about my experiences, if you *do* get upset from some of the things I have written and it motivates you to do something about it, then *good*—this book has done its job.

It is my hope that *every parent, teacher, student,* and *community stakeholder* gets riled up about something within these pages and is motivated to do something about it in their respective community. Our kids deserve better than the mundane and mediocre educational experiences many of them have had and are having. Let's keep the conversation going and start a movement to make change in our skoolz nationwide.

Email me at skoolzrdumb@gmail.com and together let's find ways to exchange ideas and start making things better for our kids (or if you are a student, which is even better, use this book as fuel to improve circumstances for you and your peers in the present). Our time is now, and the moment couldn't be more perfect.

For those of you whose schools are *not* dumb, where all of the teachers are overflowing with excitement and love for their jobs and the students are having topnotch, unforgettable experiences that will allow them to achieve their wildest dreams, I would like to challenge you. Perhaps everything in your school is close to perfect and checks all the boxes. If by chance, this is your experience, let's collaborate and see how we can scale and replicate those schools all over the United States and possibly even the world.

AFTERWORD

One of my goals as a teacher was to be able to teach the things that a lesson plan and subject-area curricula couldn't teach. My time in the classroom was short, but it is my hope that this book serves as an extension of my teaching, and reaches many more people because I am not limited to a small group of students within the confines of a classroom. This book is like a power bank of life lessons I have compiled to help keep you charged.

I am always amazed to see how people in my age group (and often older), use apps that don't require much battery power but constantly work to ensure that our mobile devices are adequately charged. We also have chargers and/or power banks on hand if our batteries get low. By contrast, younger people tend to utilize battery-draining apps until they are critically low in battery power with no hopes for a charger in sight. They always wait until the very last percentage to start scrambling for a cord, brick, or power bank to give them a boost. Or, they find a cheap cord that may give the battery a little boost to begin with, but that eventually burns the battery out. This is similar to the way people access wisdom in their lives: older people are often drawing upon wisdom for all they do and try to have it on hand when it's needed for a variety of circumstances. Young people, on the other hand, don't always have wisdom at their disposal to help guide them through processes and situations, and even when they do, they only seek or ask for it when they reach critical moments in their lives. Unfortunately, some never seek it at all, or seek out wisdom from the wrong places (cheap cords/chargers) and they "die"—either literally through suicide, addictions to a variety of substances, or self-harming behaviors or figuratively by giving up on their hopes and dreams. I know this feeling. There was a point in my life in which I felt I had no purpose—I was empty and not living up to my full potential. There are messages—good, bad, and ugly—that come from what we have endured during the thirteen years of our lives from kindergarten to our senior year in high school: "You're smart." "You're dumb." "You're too smart for this." "You're not smart enough for that." If you're not careful, these messages will consume you and you begin to embody them without understanding that you are a whole human that exists without the definitions and expectations skoolz can put on you.

We spend the majority of our young lives in school and, as a result, our experiences within schools sometimes define what we think about ourselves and how we operate in the world around us. Shortly after I graduated from college, I didn't have a steady job and really didn't know what I wanted to do. Unfortunately, I fell victim to school's definitions of my talents and abilities, but I struggled to figure out how I could convert those skills into a career path I could thrive in. President of the National Honor Society didn't lead me on the fast track to the C-suite. Captain of the track team didn't land me a coaching position. Graduating from high school with a higher than 4.0 GPA didn't have job recruiters knocking my doors down with offers. I didn't continue these endeavors in my college years so there was no bridge to what I had done in my past to connect me to a successful future. Without that bridge, all of my K-12 educational experiences as a smart and influential leader fell into a sea of disillusion and doubt and I almost drowned. My light went dim, and my power was extinguished. I had used up my battery power and was seeking a charge but could never find the right outlet. I almost ran out of power completely—my battery percentage was low, even though my capacity for power was high. As I wrestled with understanding my purpose, there was a nagging in my soul and a "call"—not faint, but just audibly enough for me to know I needed to answer it. Answering that call led me back to my source—school, which has ultimately led me to this book.

Within these pages, I have admitted my failures, evaluated the parts of my educational journey that didn't go the way I wanted to, admitted the role I played in my own setbacks, and asked for forgiveness from those who I mistreated, blamed, or let down along the way. In some ways, this book has been painful and cathartic for me to write, but it is my hope that through my hardships, you are blessed with relief. As you navigate in, through, and eventually out of school, in whatever capacity that may be, may this book serve as a power bank of wisdom for whenever you need to replenish your battery life . . .

May you never lose your charge—stay powerful, my friends!

ACKNOWLEDGMENTS

When I first started writing this book, I was angry, frustrated, and fed up with the educational system. It was the middle of the sheltering-in-place period of the Covid-19 pandemic and I hated the way skoolz were choosing to operate. I was teaching at a charter school and it was difficult for me to navigate teaching other kids remotely while also working with my own four children. It was during this time that all the thoughts and ideas I had about schools came flooding into my brain. They got mixed in with all the frustrations I was having as a teacher during Covid-19 and *Skoolz R Dumb* was conceived.

It has taken me over four years to complete the writing process for various reasons, but here we are. There are so many people who were instrumental in bringing this book to fruition and I am so thankful for their prayers, encouragement, support, and input. To be honest, this book is the result of a higher calling, so I have to give honor to God. There's no way I could have had the discipline and flowing of ideas to put in this book if I were not divinely led to do this work. There is a concept throughout the book *The Alchemist* by Paulo Coehlo that I believe sums up how this book came into being: "When you are attempting to accomplish your personal legend, the entire universe will conspire to help you achieve it." Thank you to all of my co-conspirators in helping me achieve the writing and publishing of this book.

Words cannot and will never be able to adequately express the gratitude I have for my family.

My parents, Ann and Wallace, who have loved me unconditionally through all of my trials and triumphs—my amazing accomplishments and my maniacal mistakes—and for always being there for me, no matter what. Thank you for your constant and consistent support. Financially, you sacrificed your savings to help provide me with resources. Emotionally, you nudged me through the writing process. As parents, you gave me the best possible foundation a child could have. I took for granted some of your wisdom and made my fair share of mistakes, many of which are outlined in this book. But I hope that you know that I could not have asked for better parents. Together, the both of you raised us to be the very best versions of ourselves, and I am forever grateful for the love you infused in us, allowing us to have an overflow of love to share with others.

My "little big brother," Ryan, who has been my Day One since day one. I appreciate you for forever having my back, opening doors of opportunity for me and my babies, and pushing me forward, even when you didn't know you were doing so. I trust your judgment and wisdom and I'm grateful that when I asked if you wanted to read parts of the book, you said, "I just can't wait to hold it in my hand," so that I could continue to work to get it published. I hope I have made you proud.

My husband, Shakeer, whose love for me has transcended time, distance, religion, and circumstances. You have accepted, appreciated, and agape-loved me for all that I am since the day we first met, and I will be forever thankful to you for being who you are and allowing me to be who I am. You have been my sounding board, my shoulder to cry on, and throughout the writing of this book, you were my thesaurus, dictionary, research advisor, wordsmith, and editor. You never doubted my ability to get this done and have been my inspiration long before I even started writing this book. I am so blessed, and I thank God (Allah) for you. I love you!!!

My babies—you endured many long days in which I was away from home to write this book, and I appreciate your patience and support, and for allowing me to share some of your experiences with the world with hopes that we can improve education for all. You are extraordinary children, and I am so proud to be your mother. I do not know what I could have done to receive such a privilege, but I am truly honored, blessed, and thankful for all of you. My love for you is immeasurable and I appreciate the love you reciprocate to me.

Jo—thank you for believing in me and always encouraging me to "go be great" while being my authentic self and "speak my truth." You are (and have always been) wise beyond your years and I am always in awe of you.

Meena—I am thankful for your hugs and kind words. You keep me lifted up and bless me with your authenticity and boldness, wrapped in your quiet, loving spirit.

Ray—I thank you for blessing me with your presence—it is truly a gift. When everyone else stays home, you roll with me and we have built an unbreakable bond. I know you are happy that this book is finished so that you and I can hang out freely without me being distracted with the writing process. I appreciate you more than you could ever know.

Jibs—thank you for blessing me with your genuine adoration and care. I am so grateful for your love and excitement—it makes my heart smile and the feeling is mutual.

I often thank God for my in-laws and wonder what I did to be married into such an amazing family. You are some of the most wonderful human beings I know, and I am so grateful for all of you. To my parents-in-love—Ummi Khadijah, Bro. Idris, Abu Jibril, Ummi Amra, Um Dhameerah, and the late "Wali" Malik, thank you for raising such phenomenal people and welcoming me into your hearts and your family. To Sulaiman and Selamawit, Dhaamin and Barb, Jameelah, Daoud, Jathiya and Aquil, Saffiyah and Matt, Hussain and

Nafisah, Reyhanna, Ateeq and Jean, Abdur, Hassan and Teresa, Yusef and Nicole, Isa, Najwa, Junaid, Malik, Yasmine and Ousman, Naheelah, Ayeesha, Khris and Shanise, Zaynab, Stacy, and Jada—thank you so much for sharing your brother with me and for being the additional siblings that I could only dream of. I never could have imagined being loved as a sister so beautifully by so many and I am beyond thankful for all of your love and support.

Aunt Carla, Camille, and Uncle Chris—you have known about this book since its inception and I thank you for believing in me. Cousin Chelle—thank you for always checking in on us.

Inda—how blessed I am that you and Ryan chose each other. Thank you for being a wonderful sister and for your love, support, and constant positivity. Through you, I have also had the privilege to be blessed with "bonus parents" in Mrs. Ida, Mr. Tate, and David. You are all so amazing and I appreciate all of you.

To "my crew"—through track, we became teammates, but our love for each other made us sisters and forever friends and you are my extended family. Shadana and Trey, Charlene and Victor, Lisa and Craig, Charmaine, and Toya. You have been encouraging me to write a book since we were in college. Thank you for believing in me and planting the seed for me to even think I could bring forth a written work in this form. Now that *I* see myself as a writer, there will be much more of my writing to come. Shadana, I fully expect you to publish your creative works for the stage and the screen. Your storytelling gift is incredible and the world deserves to experience it—let's get it, Sis!!!

Kelli and Chason, Jacquie and Isadore, Pat, Adra, Tanshea, Dana, Mikayla, Anisa, Mrs. Sameerah—thank you and your families for holding me down in a strange place and becoming an extension of my family when I was so far away from home. Your love for me and my family helped carry me through the long cold winters and I am beyond grateful for our friendship and sisterly love.

Mrs. Sano—I cannot thank you enough for being there to care for my babies so that I could take advantage of the many opportunities that inspired the writing of this book. Your love for children is immeasurable and I'm so thankful that mine were blessed to be in your care when I couldn't take them with me. Ms. Robin—you set the tone with my oldest baby, and I am thankful for your care of him.

Nikki, Tonya R, Myra, AJ, Kenitra, Renee, and Eva—your neighborly friendship and encouragement is sublime.

Tish—you were there for me in the beginning and helped with the ideas that started this book. Thank you for inspiring me even when you didn't even know you were doing so.

Kendra, Leah, Amika, Keenan, Kristy, Charmaine GW, Chavonne, Ty, David, Kim, Steve, Adia, Andre, Derrick the "Entietainer," and Sho—your wisdom, friendship, and encouragement helped get me to the finish line. Thank you so much for letting me share some of my ideas with you, for reciprocating with great ideas in return, and for keeping me lifted up. Stacey—when I was struggling with Chapter 6, you helped guide me in another direction and I appreciate you for that. I hope that I did well by you and by other teachers. Daena—thank you for helping me keep my head screwed on straight when I thought I was losing it! You all are my fam, and I am so thankful for you!

Queen B—you were instrumental in helping me get over the hump, helping me know that I am worthy, helping me know that through our shared experiences we could build a bond that has the power to help us heal, and through the gift of words we have the power to heal others.

Carla, Caroline, Nikolai, Dr. Carla, Yvette, Rachel, Bettina, Janelle, Myrna, Roxane (with one "n"), Maurice, Jelani, Toni, and Rea—thank you for sharing your professional expertise and serving as my role models throughout this process. You are my "she-roes" and heroes—accomplished and nationally-recognized writers, publishers, and educators—who took your time to pour into me and I do not take that for granted. I truly appreciate you for your sage advice.

MJ—your consistent and powerful prayers and presence have helped guide me through the many challenges and triumphs I have experienced over the years since 2020. DJ—your daily "inspirational vitamins" help get my day started (and going) in the right way. Adria—thank you for being on the call, sharing your wins and woes, and helping my week get started in a "Million Dollar Way."

Emma and Julie—thank you for helping me stay "awoke" and giving me a platform to advocate for those of us suffering with sleep disorders.

Tonya (T-Bird), Viv, KT, Kendra, Kameese, Jonathan, Tommie, Terrence, Erskine, Toneka, Damiyan and Lanita, Brandi, Ikle, Audrey, Selvin, Taylor, Sidney, Kevin (Tic), Charita, Shone, Annquinette, Carolyn, Mike, Tommie, Alicia, Johnetha, Dana, Therman, Jemmerio and Terri, Del, Emmett and Tasha, Claude, Brian, Rod, Lisa, Kenny, Apryl, Dave, Marcel, Chris, Charles, Calvin, Rodregus, George, Karmen, Keith S., and Keith B.—you have been my close friends, cousins, and extended "brothers" and "sisters" for a very long time and I'm so thankful for our lifelong connection.

To Aunt Jessie, Aunt Olive, Aunt Winnie, Aunt Betty, Mrs. Ingram, Ms. Hightower, Ms. Quzack, Mr. Fred, my late Uncle Bill, Uncle Bob, Harriet, Ronita, Rod, Michelle and Morio, Tashia, Maggie, my late Aunt Helen (whose educational legacy lives on through her grandchildren Shay, Rizz, and Mitty), and Ken. Thank you for being my parent's village and the village that has provided me with so much love, encouragement, wisdom, and support since before I was born.

To my childhood BFF, Larissa, whose stories I read all the way up until the sixth grade. You are an incredible storyteller, and I am still looking forward to reading your books in our adult years. Some people might say we are getting old, but I say we just have a little more seasoning . . . it's never too late!!! I can't wait to read *your* books soon!!!

To My "Garden Club" Friends—for helping to make my junior high days into my best school years.

To the best coworkers—EVER. You are the "awesome sauce" and it is an honor to work alongside you every day. It is your passion and love for students that makes our workplace successful and helps to produce trailblazing individuals that make the world a better place.

To the parents of all my kids' friends—you are amazing and are raising phenomenal children. I am so blessed that my kids are friends with your kids and I'm so thankful that you embrace my babies as your own.

To *all* of my family members (shout out to my cousins from Columbus, Georgia, Chicago, Miami, and the DMV) and friends (who are like family to me) who have encouraged the writing of this book and given me the inspiration to keep going, thank you.

To Pastor PT and Bishop DC, thank you for answering God's call on your life, serving as His vessel, and for pouring into me and countless others. Allowing Him to speak through you has been instrumental in getting me to the finish line with this book!!!

Although I have attempted to do so, I am so sorry I am unable to thank everyone individually. However, if I know you in real life or on social media and you have shared an encouraging word or comment, look, word, text message, a hug, or even prayed for me as I have endured this process, I am grateful for you and I could not have written this book without your help.

Thank you to all of the classroom teachers I had from kindergarten to twelfth grade. Some of you are mentioned in chapter 6—Teachers R . . . Whether your name is mentioned during that chapter (or not) and regardless of my experience with you, I am grateful for the impact you had on my life and how you helped shape me into the person I have become. I am forever thankful for you!

There is a "Power in Place" and because of my small home with many people, I had to find different places outside of my home in which I could write. During my writing time, I learned to have a great appreciation for coffee shops, especially those that held space for me and gave me a welcoming space for me to create and bring forth this work. Those places are as follows:

404 Coffee in South Atlanta

Coffee Man in Hapeville

Kupcakerie in East Point

Lee and White in the West End

Portrait Coffee in the West End

Sangster's Café in Powder Springs

Urban Grind in Midtown

C'est La Vie Café in College Park

Black Coffee in Atlanta

Along this journey, small, independent bookstores have also served as inspiration to the completion of this book and I appreciate their value to the communities they serve. The ones I visited, with visions of having this book on their shelves are:

44th and 3rd (Atlanta, GA)

A Cappella Books (Atlanta, GA)

The Book Worm Bookstore (Powder Springs, GA)

Brave and Kind Bookstore (Decatur, GA)

Jubilee Books (inside of Kupcakerie, East Point, GA)

Medu Bookstore (Atlanta, GA)

Nubian Books (Morrow, GA)

Posman Books (Atlanta, GA)

Third House Books (Gainesville, FL)

The Lynx Bookstore (Gainesville, FL)

Book Club (New York, NY)

1804 Books (New York, NY)

There are many organizations and institutions whose support and infrastructure made way for many of the experiences that have inspired me to make a difference in education. I am thankful for all that they have done and are doing to change the world for the better and for having a part in bringing this book to fruition:

AAMBC/Black Writers Weekend, founded by Tamika Jamison. Thank you for creating a platform for this book to be discovered. I am so grateful for you and this incredible organization!!!

African American Babies Coalition (AABC)

African American Leadership Forum (AALF)

Big Picture Learning

Birth Equity Community Council (BECC)

Black Men Teach

The Bush Foundation

Coalition for Asian American Leadership (CAAL)

EdAllies

Education Evolving, (Twin Cities, MN)

Education Reimagined

Educators 4 Excellence (Also known as E4E)

GeorgiaCan

Integrated Care for High-Risk Pregnancies (ICHRP)

iNACOL

Knowledgeworks

MinnCan

The Minneapolis Foundation

MnEEP

Network for the development of Children of African Descent (NdCAD)

Wilder Foundation

2 Revolutions

The 74

Joscelyn—thank you for the design work that created the graphics to be just as unique as the book itself and for helping me establish my brand.

To the staff at BookLogix . . . thank you for believing in me. Thank you for thinking enough of this book to publish it. Thank you for all your edits, design work, formatting, and patience with me through this process. Thank you for making me a part of the BookLogix family. Thank you for bringing *Skoolz R Dumb* to life!

REFERENCES

http://joe-bower.blogspot.com/2012/09/a-short-history-of-grading.html

https://en.wikibooks.org/wiki/Foundations_of_Education_and_Instructional_Assessment/Grading/Purpose?wprov=srpw1_0

https://ajc.tumblr.com/post/51057535695/william-farish-the-worlds-most-famous-lazy

Page 62

https://www.gadoe.org/External-Affairs-and-Policy/communications/Pages/PressReleaseDetails.aspx?PressView=default&pid=904

Page 63

https://www.bizjournals.com/orlando/news/2018/12/03/hoping-to-land-a-sports-scholarship-ucf-is-best.html

https://www.collegesimply.com/colleges/florida/university-of-central-florida/salaries/

https://nypost.com/2021/09/01/donald-de-la-haye-quit-college-football-now-hes-a-youtube-millionaire/

https://naibuzz.com/how-much-money-deestroying-makes-on-youtube-net-worth/

www.ingramcontent.com/pod-product-compliance
Lightning Source LLC
Chambersburg PA
CBHW052137070526
44585CB00017B/1864